D0543561

# People Without History

## India's Muslim Ghettos

Jeremy Seabrook and
Imran Ahmed Siddiqui

**Pluto**Press
www.plutobooks.com

First published 2011 by Pluto Press
345 Archway Road, London N6 5AA and
175 Fifth Avenue, New York, NY 10010

www.plutobooks.com

Distributed in the United States of America exclusively by
Palgrave Macmillan, a division of St. Martin's Press LLC,
175 Fifth Avenue, New York, NY 10010

British Library Cataloguing in Publication Data
A catalogue record for this book is available from the British Library

ISBN    978 0 7453 3114 0    Hardback
ISBN    978 0 7453 3113 3    Paperback

Library of Congress Cataloging in Publication Data applied for

This book is printed on paper suitable for recycling and made from fully
managed and sustained forest sources. Logging, pulping and manufacturing
processes are expected to conform to the environmental standards of the
country of origin.

10   9   8   7   6   5   4   3   2   1

Designed and produced for Pluto Press by
Chase Publishing Services Ltd, 33 Livonia Road, Sidmouth, EX10 9JB, England
Typeset from disk by Stanford DTP Services, Northampton, England
Simultaneously printed digitally by CPI Antony Rowe, Chippenham, UK
and Edwards Bros in the USA

# Contents

# Acknowledgements

This book is about life in the inner-city areas of Kolkata's poor, mainly Muslim settlements. The reason for this focus is twofold: the growing separation of Muslims in India from the Hindu mainstream; and the isolation of the poor from the image of contemporary India, which has successfully been projected to the world, embodied in cliches about the 'powerhouse of tomorrow', 'waking giant' and 'future superpower.' The rulers of India have become complacent as a result of the flattery they have received, much of it from their erstwhile imperial masters, and the fate of the poor in the euphoria of high economic growth figures has become a marginal concern. No longer responsive to injustice and inequality, the government of India appears content to attribute gratuitous malevolence to those who resist; and although the Maoists are currently the principal public enemy, Muslims are rarely far behind, since it is believed that they will not hesitate to use violence and terror as means of securing their aim – an aim which the Hindu Right sees, absurdly, distortedly, as dominance. The Muslim minority – some 150 million people – is perceived by many in India as a population of doubtful belonging and uncertain allegiance to the state.

This book is the result of an effort in which many people have participated and, although Imran Ahmed Siddiqui and Jeremy Seabrook are acknowledged as the principal authors and collaborators, it reflects the contribution of many people living and working in some of the city's most forlorn communities. It deals predominantly – though not exclusively – with areas covered by Tiljala-SHED, an organisation which has worked with the urban poor for almost three decades.[1] It does not reflect the opinions of those associated with this non-government organisation, but evokes the atmosphere of the poorest places in the city – the vulnerability, the poverty and the hopes of a majority of Kolkata's Muslims, who make up 25 per cent of the city population. Tiljala-SHED reflects both the possibilities and the limitations of what can be achieved within existing power-relationships, without changing the structural division between rich and poor. Welfare, reform and mitigation, certainly – and these mean dramatic improvements in the experience of poor people – but against the great movements of globalism and geo-political polarisation, against corruption and power, the voices of humanity and tolerance are easily drowned out.

We are grateful to Mohammad Alamgir of Tiljala-SHED, who was intermittently part of the 'we' referred to in the text. Also part of this first person plural was Haider Ali, who also grew up and has spent his 35 years in the area; Jabeen Arif, who has worked in the most wretched part of Topsia for over a decade; and Imran Ahmed Siddiqui who, like many of the residents of the inner city areas, comes from an Urdu-speaking background in Uttar Pradesh and now works with the *Telegraph* newspaper in Kolkata. We would also like to acknowledge the support of all at Tiljala-SHED, especially Salma Khatoon, Rubina Hussein and the other Haider Ali (no relation). We would like to express thanks for financial help from the Network for Social Change in producing this book, which is part of a wider project on 'Cities of Hunger'.

We are also grateful to Kamini Adhikari, Dr A. K. M. Siddiqui in Kolkata, Rifat Faridi of the Calcutta Muslim

Orphanage, Murtaza Shibli in London, and especially to the people of Topsia, Tangra, Tiljala, Beniapukur and other Muslim communities, for their generosity in sharing with us their stories of life and labour in Kolkata in 2010, their sense of distance from those who govern and, not infrequently, harass and abuse them. Theirs is indeed a life apart, largely uncelebrated and for the most part, unrecorded; which is a pity, for it illuminates the condition of those about whose lives the rich and powerful weave their cruel fantasies of terror and violence, but who, overwhelmingly, struggle, like poor people everywhere, simply to live and to survive another day.

## Note

1.  Tiljala-SHED (Tiljala Society for Human and Educational Development) was established in 1987 and registered in 1993 under the West Bengal Societies Registration Act of 1961. Its primary purpose was the improvement of the slums of Tiljala, but it has since extended its reach to a wide arc of mainly Muslim settlements in central Kolkata and its activities include slum, squatter and pavement dwellers. It has been funded by a number of European agencies including MISEREOR (Germany), which finances improvements in the conditions of rag-pickers and their families. This includes setting up a link between the corporate sector and collection of recyclable solid waste at source.

There is a sponsorship programme for the education of poor girls (supported by AIDOS from Italy – see below). The project aims at the education of girls, since this is the surest way to ensure a wider dissemination of progressive ideas in society, as well as providing protection for some of the most vulnerable in fighting exploitation, early marriage and exposure to harmful environments.

There are in addition micro-finance programmes (Trickle-Up Program), an Integrated Programme for Street Children (supported by the Indian Government Ministry of Women and Child Development), which is designed for children living on the street, beside railway lines and the banks of canals; the objective being the integration of such children into the formal education system.

Tiljala-SHED also participates in Shikshalaya Prakalpa, a government initiative to bring destitute children of primary school age into education; while the Kolkata National Child Labour Project, supported by the Ministry of Labour is to withdraw child workers from hazardous enterprises and to work towards their inclusion in the educational system. A cultural unit of T-SHED helps poor children to display their singing, acting and dancing talent.

All offers of support and help are welcome. Please contact:

TILJALA SHED
6C and 6D Rifle Range Road
Kolkata 700019
India
Tel. 0091-33-22802681 / 22817392 / 22831084
e-mail: tished@cal2vsnl.net.in
mdalamgir2001@yahoo.co.in

*Main kis kay hath pay apna lahoo talaash karoon
Tamam shehar ne pahney huay hain dastaney.*

On whose hands shall I look for my blood
When the whole city is wearing gloves?

(Ahmed Faraz, 1931–2007)

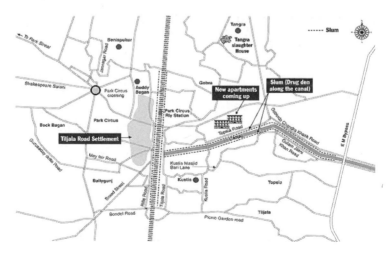

Tiljala Road (© Nilratan Maity)

# Introduction

*Taqdeer kay qazi ka hai fatwa yeh azal say*
*Hei jurm-e-zaeefi ki saza marg mafajaat*

Fate has decreed from antiquity
That those who commit the crime of powerlessness must die
(Faiz Ahmed Faiz, 1911–1984)

The non-Muslim world has become obsessed with Muslims, but almost entirely in relation to their religious identity and beliefs, especially insofar as these are perceived as 'moderate' or 'extreme'. In particular, since the attacks on the United States in 2001, Spain in 2004, Britain in 2005 and across the world including Mumbai in 2008, Muslims have been defined solely by their faith, as though this penetrated their every action and thought. This shallow, ostensibly 'spiritual', concern has had some unfortunate consequences. There is an obvious dissonance between the avowed preoccupation with 'winning hearts and minds' in Iraq, Afghanistan, Yemen and other countries where 'alienated' Muslims are believed to be found, and the disregard for everything that relates to the heart and mind of actually existing humanity. This response is counter-productive, because it omits most areas of experience in which the common interests of Muslims and all other human beings might be affirmed and strengthened. It is as though there were a specifically Islamic inflection in every daily action that sets them apart, so that there is a distinctive way of laughing and sleeping; a Muslim sensibility in work, in the affections, in pleasure; a peculiarly Muslim form of speaking, walking or weeping.

One thing clear in the poorest Muslim communities of Kolkata is that the people there have much to weep about; although the circumstances which prompted their tears also affect many people who live in the unvisited slum settlements of the world – the tears of sorrow and anger of the mother whose son, a simple electrician, was falsely and knowingly accused by the security services of being the 'mastermind' behind blasts in Varanasi and elsewhere in 2007, and whose maternal tenacity prevailed against the power of the Indian state; the synthetic tears of the young man, hooked on the heroin-derived 'brown sugar', requesting money for 'rehabilitation' which would only feed his addiction; the tears of joy of the father who learned that his daughter had been accepted on a teacher training course; the tears of grief of the old woman whose elderly cycle-rickshaw husband had been killed when the barrier of a level crossing came down across his back; the tears of frustration of the graduate who, unable to find work, had spent a lifetime recycling scrap plastic and who now sees his son, newly qualified, in the same position 25 years later. For all these people, secular survival was an overwhelming priority and in the often desperate search for livelihood, however pious they may have been, little time remained to them for the contemplation of eternity.

Little attention has been paid to the fabric of daily life in poor Muslim communities – the pursuit of gainful occupation, affective and social affinities, networks of kinship and neighbourhood. Small notice has been taken of those aspects of life which unite all human societies; omissions which suggest the wilful creation of a fictive enemy, rather than the extensive hostility that Muslims in general are supposed to harbour against people of other faiths.

Although this book is focussed on India, the evidence it provides is no less relevant to Europe and other countries in which Muslims make up a sizeable minority of the population – Thailand, the Philippines, Ethiopia, as well as Britain, France and the Netherlands. Is this a consequence of neglect, or of a perverse construction of shadow-enemies without which, it seems, human societies are unable to define themselves to their own satisfaction? Whatever the answer to that, there is a widespread view that little common ground exists between Muslims and the rest of humanity. This has become axiomatic for many politicians and leaders of the world, and, perhaps surprisingly, also of many intellectuals who contrast our 'progress' with their 'backwardness'. These preconceptions not only deny the sameness of human concerns everywhere, but also block pathways to tolerant and peaceable amity between peoples.

The book is intended as a small corrective to this unhappy state of affairs, since it asks a simple question; how do the vast majority of Muslims, especially the poor, live, work, love and die? During the period we spent in the predominantly Muslim areas of Kolkata, we were treated with kindness and sympathy, and found everywhere the generosity of spirit of the poor, which stands in such contrast to the grudging retentiveness of wealth. What swiftly became apparent was that survival and livelihood were of greater urgency to them than any inquiry into the spiritual condition of the urban poor. How do you labour, where do you find security and shelter, and how do you confront the vicissitudes of everyday life? How do you live with neighbours and family, and what is your response to labour rewarded at rates below subsistence, unemployment, untreated sickness and the multiple hungers that torment the deprived of the world? We were asking these questions of the poorest people in Kolkata; and that is saying something, in spite of recent official efforts to 'beautify' the city, to 'modernise' its economy and to colonise poverty by removing poor people from the city centre and constructing monumental towerblocks for an assertive middle class.

Muslims are heavily concentrated in the *basti*[1] areas adjacent to the commercial and business centre of Kolkata. In this inner-ring area, they constitute a minority in at least three ways. First of all, to be Muslim is to be a member of a community against which discrimination and prejudice are part of daily experience. These particular Muslims are also a minority by virtue of the fact that they are Urdu speakers among Bengalis. Some migrated from Bihar, Orissa and Uttar Pradesh at the time when Kolkata, in the imperial twilight, was still the second city of the British Empire; others in the dawn-promise of Independence, when the city still held out a prospect of hope and livelihood to the famished landless. They worked in the port and docks, as 'coolies' (a word from the Turkish *quli*, or 'slave'), in artisanal occupations (now often archaic and unprofitable) in which they were skilled, in factories and industrial enterprises that have since become defunct. Many are now stranded in poverty, performing some of the most degrading labour in the city: rickshaw-drivers, maidservants, workers in plastic and rubber, in construction and transport, and above all, in the vast labour of recycling every conceivable used-up commodity. All the detritus of the city passes through their hands, in an epic work which wastes nothing but the perishable flesh and blood of the people.

A majority of the people of Bengal were Muslim before Partition. The decision of most in the Eastern part of Bengal to become part of Pakistan at the time of Independence (what became Bangladesh in the Liberation War of 1971) left, in West Bengal, a Hindu-majority state that was, in effect, a truncated Bengal, although it contained Calcutta (now Kolkata), the former imperial capital of India.

The third aspect of the minority status of Kolkata's Muslims is that they are urban, whereas the majority of Muslims in West Bengal live in rural areas. The fact that they retain the language and customs of Bihar and Uttar Pradesh is the most eloquent comment on their sense of separation, not fully integrated into the life either of the city or of the state of West Bengal.

There is yet another significant factor in the lives of city Muslims. They have been in a city governed by the Communist Party of India (Marxist) for 33 years, until May 2010 when the local administration was toppled by Mamata Banerjee's Trinamool Congress Party. It has been the proudest boast of the Communists, that they have been guided by a secular ideology, and that, as a result, Muslims in West Bengal have been spared the excesses of communalists in Gujarat, Maharashtra, Orissa and elsewhere. How far this claim is justified may be judged from the testimonies of the people in this book.

The circumstances of their lives create constant insecurity. This generates social and cultural conservatism, and makes for inturned communities, apart and fretful, qualities that inhibit the growth and development of its members, makes them distrust outsiders and, indeed, turns them into victims of those who, astonishingly, manage to make money out of people who have almost nothing.

If poverty truly were a major generator of terror, as many world leaders regularly assert, these areas of Kolkata might be its principal breeding-ground, and the world would already be in a far more advanced state of destructive ruin than anything we have seen. Poverty does not create extremism, at least not among the poor themselves. The vast majority of the people show tireless energy only in their attempts to make a living that will support them and those they love. It is not that what are euphemistically called 'anti-social elements' are absent: unemployment is high and there are always groups of young men, grimly watchful of any opportunity for gain, ready to be recruited by gangs controlled by politicians, developers and the police. But these are greatly outnumbered by their peers, the young men who sit for twelve-hour days in chappal-making units (makers of basic shoes, mostly slippers, consisting of sole and an upper, with strips of material for the toes), performing tasks of unimaginable tedium, in overwhelming heat, and in the mild euphoria-inducing smell of adhesive, cutting, shaping, gluing and trimming shoes sufficient for the feet of a whole world.

There will, of course, be other objections to the stories told by people in this book, apart from the obvious one – that they disconfirm the dangerous ignorance of the powerful of the world. For it seems that most people prefer myths, stories and narratives that support their prejudices rather than acknowledging more prosaic social realities that might disappoint their sense of drama. How much more comforting it is to excite oneself with lurid imaginings than to make the brief trip into vilified communities, and to risk discovering there that the fantasies are without substance!

India's recently-acquired position as a major economic power has infected the middle class with strange exaltations; so that anyone who now speaks of the poverty of India is felt to be betraying this new essence of the country, the transformation which has struck the begging-bowl from the skinny hands of the poor and substituted for it the fleshy wellbeing of Bollywood, and the unstable flicker of the computer screen. Any depiction of the 400 million or so poor (actually nobody knows how many people remain poor, and even definitions of poverty have become elusive and contradictory) is now usually denounced as 'poverty porn', while the flamboyant excesses of the rich – the multi-million dollar weddings, the 28-storey mansions, the establishment of a dedicated air corridor for private helicopters – are seen not for the obscenity they are, but as tokens of India's arrival at the 'top tables' of the world.

The one-sided admiration for the economic success of today's India is so pervasive that it leaves little space for anything so disturbing as an actual portrayal of the social and economic position of Dalits (victims of the caste system), Adivasis (tribal people, the original inhabitants of India, whose ancestral lands so inconveniently bestride mineral resources urgently required for 'development') and, of course, a majority of Muslims. The reports of the Sachar Committee[2] and the Misra Commission[3] described the systematic economic and social deprivation of Muslims, and their exclusion from places of influence and power, created a momentary flurry of recognition, before being swallowed up in the bureaucratic torpor of laissez-faire. It is significant in this regard that West Bengal proved to have one of the worst records for the representation of Muslims in the administration and the bureaucracy.

The myths surrounding India's largest minority are not easily dispelled, locked as they are into geo-political prejudices shared by many in Europe, the United States and other places where Muslims constitute a significant minority. Religious and social cliches merge: Muslims, the story goes, especially young Muslims, are vulnerable to brain-washing, and their transformation into terrorists is achieved by a conviction that if they sacrifice their lives, they will go straight to paradise to be consoled by 72 virgins (I lost count of the number of times this solemn affirmation was made to me by knowing Hindus, who thought they were initiating me into a wisdom barely within my grasp).

Muslims have large families[4] and are polygamous, in a self-conscious conspiratorial attempt to 'out-breed' the majority. Muslims are anti-national and anti-social: interpreted, this means that those who are not criminals are intent upon subverting the state. Muslims refuse to 'integrate'. Muslims allow archaic notions of faith to interfere with the necessities of economic and social life. They are their own worst enemies, denying education to their girls and oppressing women. These harsh fancies thrive on segregation and a particular kind of gilded unknowing, of which the most instructed and well-off are such expert practitioners.

It would be foolish to imagine that such cherished convictions are amenable to reason. But whatever happens in India and the world, it cannot be claimed that no one was aware of the disabilities and privations to which Muslims have been subjected, and the humiliations to which their daily life is both witness and reproach. The ordinary lives recounted here tell how things are with poor Muslims; their sufferings, but also their ambitions, their desire for stability and sufficiency, and their often thwarted faith in education and improvement. That they are accessory to their own misery may offer comfort to those who regard oppression and dominance as the natural order of the world; but this has nothing to do with the quiet efforts of most people in these desolate places to transcend obstacles to human, as well as social and economic, emancipation.

# 1
# Topsia

*Humko halaat ki sooli pe chadhanay walo*
*Humnay har haal mein jeenay ki kasam khayee hai*

Let those who have led us to the noose of Time know
We have vowed to live through every calamity

## I

## THE LANDSCAPE

The area of Topsia in Kolkata was, until recently, portrayed on city maps as a blank space, marked only by the words 'liable to inundation'. Slums, trackless and impermanent, have no geography.

They have no history either. They exist for a brief moment, a fugitive humanity, in city spaces; people who come from nowhere and subsequently vanish into thin air. Either the slum gains official recognition by the city authorities and evolves – often slowly and painfully – into a 'community', or it is razed unceremoniously by police and municipal employees, and the people are dispersed to the four winds.

Part of Topsia has developed into a dense mesh of high-rise buildings, so close together they can scarcely breathe. These are mostly illegal structures, erected by collusion between politicians and 'developers', and although small apartments may still be bought for as little as 150,000 rupees ($3000), properties on the ground floor are far more expensive since they can be turned into shops or units for manufacturing goods, especially shoes, the rudimentary chappals (the most common employment of poor Muslims in Kolkata). Topsia has, in the past few years, become a vast building site: chaotic, unplanned and unauthorised, towers of cement now loom over the remaining self-built slum areas, threatening to claim for the market as real estate land that has long been occupied by those sometimes referred to as 'marginal populations'.

But the poorest district in Topsia is an elongated island between two canals of waste water, about a kilometre in length. There are two parallel rows of huts, each overlooking a polluted waterway, the smell of which is so overpowering you can taste it. I thought of Ivan Illich who, in 1986 described 'the smell of development – the stench of dwelling space that has begun to decay.'[5] The water rushes through a concrete sluice-gate, a toxic waterfall of industrial effluent and sewage. 'The Pollution Board', one resident said, 'does not see this dirty water. But they banned the book fair on the Maidan close to the Victoria Monument, because it killed the grass. Trampling people is apparently more acceptable than treading on the grass.'

The huts typically rise to a height of about one and a half metres. Their relative uniformity suggests they were not constructed by the present occupants, but by political parties that had an interest in re-locating people evicted from elsewhere. This is confirmed by the residents, many of whom were displaced by one of the frequent fires that sweep through the slums. On the land they formerly occupied new apartments are rising.

The huts have frames of bamboo and wood, walls of *chetai* (woven strips of bamboo), polythene, tin and industrial detritus. Roofs are either tiled or weighted down against the wind by bricks, stones and old bicycle tyres. Some people have constructed an earthen dam at the threshold, while others rely on a high wooden bed as a refuge against monsoon floodwater. A tin trunk (evidence of the elsewhere from which they migrated, sometimes long ago), metal folding chairs, plastic cans for drinking water, a few basic utensils, a clay stove, a change of shabby clothing – these are people's total possessions. It is difficult to imagine a humanity more bereft than these unacknowledged refugees in the heart of an Indian metropolitan city.

People are used up by malnutrition, untreated sickness, exploitative labour and drugs. A young woman wheels a cart bearing a few specked apples; another carries rotting oranges and blackened bananas – the closest thing to luxury in this forsaken place. Small shops offer sweets and *bidis*, pastries in plastic bags hung out of the reach of rats. There is little sign of more substantial food stores, but there are at least five drug dens.

If the idea of a 'drug den' is an anachronism – evoking Limehouse or San Francisco in the late nineteenth century – what goes on inside them is very contemporary. A shabby curtain hangs at the entrance, and inside, on the floor of beaten earth or a wooden extension built over the swollen waters, small groups of young men are chasing the dragon: they place a pellet of heroin onto a silver foil, melt it into a brownish transparent liquid with a match held beneath the foil and inhale the fumes through a cylinder of silver paper. The only social interaction between them is providing one another with the flame; apart from that, they are locked in lonely dreams of transcendence. The quality of the heroin cannot be very high – each portion costs 40 rupees (less than $1).

There is no concealment of this, or any other, substance abuse. Dealers move in and out of the huts clutching a thickening bundle of 100-rupee notes; a woman squats at a doorstep, folding money into the knotted end of her saree. Although drugs are allowed on credit, no one is permitted to default. A young man with a limp, a bandaged arm and hand in a splint, sustained his injuries when attacked by dependants of the druglord because he could not pay for merchandise he had already used. Drugs are a pitiless business: they consume youth and energy, which evaporate here as swiftly as the fumes from the intoxicants. After dark, the area springs to even more vibrant life, since this is the destination of addicts from all over the city; a world of shadow-people, some of them the sons of wealth, who come here to pursue their own path of self-destruction. In the dens, the greatest fear is not that I might be a representative of the law but that I might be a journalist and therefore more likely to disturb their addiction by disclosures to the 'wrong people', who are most certainly not the city authorities.

## II
## UNTREATED SICKNESS

Scenes of degradation in Topsia are reminiscent of the foulest places in the cities of early nineteenth-century Britain. Some people, weakened by malnutrition, are shaking with fever; lying on hard wooden bedsteads and thin bedrolls on a beaten earth floor, with eyes glittering and foreheads burning. Malaria is widespread, immune systems have been ruined, and tuberculosis, that other version of consumption that mocks the heedless appetites of the urban middle class, eats up the flesh of the poor.

People carry with them, wrapped for protection in a piece of transparent polythene, prescriptions for medicines they cannot afford as well as X-rays, scans and images of the growth within – the untreated injury, the damaged organ. The mother of a rickshaw driver shows me the X-ray of his blind eye. This is not the result of a visitation of nature, but of an attack upon him. A thief had been caught by a crowd of people in the neighbourhood. They were beating the wrongdoer and, to deflect their anger, the criminal pointed to the innocent rickshaw driver as his accomplice; the crowd then turned its inflamed attention upon him. As a result of the beating, he lost the sight of an eye. This man is now in the same hospital to which his daughter was admitted two days earlier, suffering from rickets. His mother is herself shaking with malarial fever; she sits, wan and shivering, wrapped in a grey blanket on the threshold of the hut. Behind her, a grandson lies on rough bedding, exhausted by jaundice, his eyes bright yellow.

Nearby, an elderly man, Sheikh Siddiqui, whose spine was crushed by a metal pole that fell on him while he was driving his rickshaw, sits on his bed, his face contorted with pain. He wears only a faded blue *lungi* tied in a knot at the waist. His chest hair is white, his abdomen concave. He is utterly dependent upon Salima Khatoon, his wife. She is herself an old woman, who buys half-burned coal from restaurants before cleaning and selling it for fuel. She earns between 20 and 25 rupees a day ($0.50). They have one daughter who is married and lives 'near Delhi', they say, with the desolation with which people speak of the dead. And indeed, she says, daughters do not belong to their parents, but are borrowed from the future family into which they will marry. Salima Khatoon's family used to live in a room in the city, but the landlord gave her mother money to leave. She has been in Topsia for 20 years. Sometimes restaurants also give her leftover food, which supplements the poor quality rice and vegetables her thin earnings provide.

## III
## POVERTY – A CONSTANT COMPANION

Poverty is not static. It is not even a condition. It is a busy scavenger, always changing its shape, ingenious at devising new ways of robbing people of what little they possess. Poverty is an opportunistic thief, appearing now in the guise of fever or sickness, then as disability or grief, loss of occupation, homelessness and mental infirmity. It is also a tenacious companion, reluctant to let go. It pursues those to whom it is attached so that even when they flee its unwanted attentions, they find they have an appointment with it at their destination – when they run from the depleted countryside and broken farm to the provincial town or capital city, they discover it lying in wait, ready to reclaim them. Perhaps this is why it is so easy to represent poverty as Fate, and why existential woes readily merge with socially created ills.

Descriptions of what it means to be poor are often misleading, both over a lifetime and in day-to-day experience. Here, families with young children are likely to be poor, but as these begin to labour, poverty is lessened. Child labour is not seen by them as an abuse of their young, but as the only way to enhance their means of survival. When those same children come of age, marry and start their own families, poverty seizes them once more until a new generation is old enough to be set to work. In old age, too, poverty returns, and it is only in brief spells – young adulthood, and again when the children are married off – that periods of respite can be expected.

When I went back to Topsia after a period of three months, Salima Khatoon's husband had died.

> After his accident, he tried to hide it. For a long time, he didn't tell me, because he thought I would fall sick if I knew he had a problem. He continued to work, in spite of the pain and the effort it caused him. He thought his backbone had been displaced, so I borrowed money to buy him a belt to ease the pain. We didn't know he had internal injuries to the intestines. I did everything I could for him. I even went onto the streets to beg.

Salima Khatoon never dreamed he would die before her. The only consolation – also a sad coincidence – is that her daughter has returned. The daughter's husband, in an example of the multiple misfortunes which crowd in upon the poorest, died in a traffic accident. His widow has returned to her mother's home. 'Together', she says, 'we sort ashes and burnt coal. Between us, we collect four or five kilos daily.' They sell the fuel from a mat outside the hut, at four rupees a kilo. Their joint daily income is about 20 rupees ($0.50). Neighbours sometimes feed them when they have nothing to eat. When we left her, I gave Salima Khatoon 100 rupees. Later, I was told she spent it on country liquor, an expenditure it would be hard to grudge since there is no other earthly escape for her from these scenes of poverty and loss.

On the other hand, Rashida Begum, who I had last seen shivering with malaria and wondering how she would survive if her son lost his sight, had recovered. Small and dignified, she now appeared as the alert intelligent woman she is. 'We survive, *Uparvala* [The One Above] helps us. My son is better,

although the injury will never completely heal.' She invited us
into her house, a detached structure between the two rows of
houses, where the stony path widens out a little.

> My son and his wife have three children. The baby is six months old
> and we cannot afford baby food. My son does not keep one rupee for
> himself. No one in the house goes to sleep hungry, although he often
> goes off to work with nothing.

Rashida Begum is anxious to make us understand that this
is not an environment she would have chosen had she been
in control of her fate. She is in social exile, displaced by
misfortune from familiar surroundings. If she had even a
small amount of money, she would start a business, making
and selling cakes or snacks; but there is little credit available
for the poorest, and even when there is, there are more urgent
claims on the small sums they may receive – health care, food,
rent or bribes. 'There is no security here. The government
has plans to evict the people, since it wants to beautify the
canalside. We cannot breathe freely for fear of who will come
and molest us.'

She and her family have lived here for the past three years.
Before that, she was in Park Circus, on her mother's verandah.
When their mother died, her brother took over the small
apartment and threw them out because Rashida Begum's
husband was a drunkard. She left him because he would
take no responsibility for the family and provided no money
for food.

> I heard that he was dead. I don't know. I have always worked. I have
> been to Mumbai and Goa, looking after patients in a private nursing
> home. I was not qualified, but I served as helper and companion. I
> spent three years in Mumbai with one patient.

Rashida Begum is proud that she is literate. She was educated up to Class VII in a school run by the Assemblies of God (the Indian affiliate of the Pentecostal World Assemblies of God Fellowship, which originated in the United States). 'I don't want to be in such an environment as this. If it was possible to go anywhere else, do you think I would remain here? I am helpless. I brought up my son in a better home than this, and I am afraid for the children. I pray they will not become corrupted here. I never imagined in all my life that I would have to live in such a cruel place. It is a humiliation. When I was working, I used to earn 3000–4000 rupees a month (about $75). Here we live cheaply. The rent for the hut is only 300 rupees, and we get the light free, by hooking [illegal connection]. When I see the drugs and disgrace here, I pray the children may not be touched by it. I want to protect them from evil, but my arms are not long enough.' She picks up the baby from its grubby basket and hugs it to herself, saying in English, 'Good baby, bad luck.'

Rashida Begum's moment of restored wellbeing was brief. By May 2010, she was back in hospital with breathing difficulties and a lung infection. Her daughter-in-law – wife of the injured rickshaw-driver – fears for what will become of the family if they should lose the woman who has been its principal moral and social support.

This part of Topsia has only recently been occupied. Most of the people lived on the other side of the water, on a wider stretch of land, until two years ago when the area was destroyed by fire. This now-arid island was, at that time, covered with trees and shrubs. The burned-out people were encouraged to relocate here and, within a couple of months, the whole area was denuded of vegetation and colonised by the present inhabitants.

A non-government organisation supported by Tiljala-SHED has run a school here with help from the central government, the Ministry of Human Resources. Central government recently announced it will withdraw all funding from voluntary schools, under the recently enacted Right to Education Bill. In anticipation of this, it has already ceased paying for the midday meal which the non-government organisation provided for the students. As a result, many children have ceased to attend because a nutritious meal was for many the principal attraction of school. Many former students have become visibly more malnourished since the meal was discontinued. Education is, according to the bill, to be made compulsory for all children between five and 14; but there is not the remotest chance of this reaching the starvelings of Topsia. Jabeen Arif, who has been a health worker here for eleven years, says 100 children used to get food here once a day – a mixture of dal, bulgar wheat and rice, and soya bean and potato curry;

> It seems to me the government's dislike of 'informal education' is hypocritical, since what could be more informal than a government system where the teachers don't even turn up, or fail to teach, while some even fall asleep in front of their pupils? It may be that some NGOs have misused money given by the government for food; but why should our children be punished for the wrongdoing of others?

By the edge of the stinking water, groups of unemployed men are playing cards. Others, also preoccupied with escape from these scenes of misery, are drinking *chulai*, a locally made rice-based liquor. Two or three old men – that is, in their 40s and 50s – with wispy beards and vacant eyes, are begging to feed their addiction. Their lives have been wasted in the chase of an elusive dragon.

## IV
## SELF-HARM

The most troubling spectacle is that of young people – young men, principally – who damage themselves in full view of a distracted world. The only redeeming feature is the commitment of those who work in this fractured community, pious Muslims who see what they do as an act of religious duty. For here, generally, there is little sense of religion. It is as though people had been stripped of everything, including their faith, so that all that remains is the word 'Muslim' – a category that has become, in the minds of a majority in India, synonymous with poverty and crime. This is 'secular India' in its least engaging form. If people destroy themselves, this is of small concern to outsiders. If they destroy one another, that too is acceptable. It is only when they present themselves to the world in the guise of fundamentalists, Maoists or other radicals, and turn upon wealth and power, that their activities become of interest to the State. As long as nothing disturbs the existing order, who will attend to these only nominal Muslims who are as far away from their faith as they are from organising themselves into groups that will fight for justice? You do not have to be a religious extremist or an admirer of Marxism to understand that, sooner or later, people will reach for alternatives in the search of redress for this intense disrespect for the human person.

## V
## THE COLLUSION OF ELITES

In the meantime, the injuries to people here are a matter of public indifference. It is not that no one knows what takes place. On the contrary, many people in authority know very well because it provides them with a tainted livelihood. The hut-owners, who rent their premises for the purposes of the ruin of youth, must pay their dues to the police. The dealers, too, are indebted to their social and political protectors. When a social worker informed the local councillor of what was happening, she was told to mind her own business. She turned to the police and was told, 'You have a daughter. If you value her safety, leave it and do not interfere.' It is clear that the lawless misery of the people furnishes a business opportunity to lawmakers and upholders of the law.

Other, usually unseen, social transactions also appear in this abandoned place: the continuous erosion of the substance of the poor and the long, uninterrupted flow of wealth from poor to rich becomes tangible. Incredibly, in communities that appear bereft even of basic sustenance, money nonetheless is prised from their feeble grasp and wings its way, faultless as trained birds, to its rightful owners – the manipulators and possessors of wealth. In the process, even the bodies of the poor are hollowed out – bones become visible, limbs more stringy, stomachs hollow. Here, the decorous drapery of economic 'normality' is stripped away and exchanges are seen for what they are – the naked robbery of the poor by those who never cease to enrich themselves at their expense. This symbiotic dependency of rich and poor provides the clearest reason why poverty should persist; for without it, how would the extravagances of wealth survive?

Topsia is also a place where men in particular, robbed of power, grieve for lost privilege. In the drug houses, where they articulate the fantasy in which they are trapped, they make boastful claims to the empty air. One boy says that his father owns a hotel where the rooms cost the unimaginable expense of 800 rupees a day; another claims to be related to a government minister; while a third says he is a friend of Javed Khan, a leader of the Opposition Trinamool Congress Party, which hopes, in the elections of 2011, to topple the Communist Party of India (Marxist) State government, in power for a third of a century. Here, in the haze of smoky euphoria, male supremacy is briefly restored.

## VI
## WOMEN'S WORK

Women are responsible for holding together, stitching and mending the fraying fabric of social life. Theirs is the most conspicuous work in these bleak spaces. On a narrow strip of dusty earth outside a hut, a family of three young girls aged between about eleven and 14 are cutting and trimming waste from the rubber straps that will form the toe-piece of chappals. The round thongs are mass produced by pouring rubber into a mould and a certain overspill leaves rubber flaps that must be manually removed before the V-shaped straps can be fixed to the soles of the sandals. Each girl has a round bamboo basket into which the finished articles are placed and a second basket into which she drops the trimmings. For this smoothing of the rough straps, the girls earn 90 paise (just under one rupee, less than two cents) for every dozen pairs they trim. It is immensely laborious and tedious work, but so simple that it can be performed by very young children. Karima, 14, says girls as young as seven can do it. She can complete 30 dozen pairs in a day, and in her family four members are occupied in this way. Together, they can earn over a hundred rupees. Work is not available every day. None of the girls has been to school.

They must take great care with the waste because this has to be given back to the representative of the factory owner, who carefully weighs the cut-off material which will be melted down and re-used. If the weight is 200 grams less than the average, he will cut 20 rupees ($0.50) from the amount paid to the worker. Payment is made only monthly. The middleman who distributes the work keeps a record in a small notebook of each daily delivery, how many dozen. If the number returned is less than that originally distributed, further deductions are made. The young women must go to the *godown* (warehouse) each month to collect their earnings; with three or four girls or women working in a household, each may earn 600–700 rupees a month ($15).

Other women labour as maidservants. It is telling that when they go to prosperous Hindu apartments they sometimes change the name that reveals their religious origin. Nurjehan, when she wanted to work in a middle-class block of flats, introduced herself by the Hindu name 'Bina'; and that is how she has been known ever since. The lives of domestic servants are poignant, since many must desert their own children in unguarded places, while they are summoned by the superior power of money to supervise the children of the rich, often in security-patrolled apartments and gated communities. Ruksana works as a maidservant in three houses in Ballygunge. She leaves her two daughters, aged seven and ten (who do not go to school) in the house and, although she asks the neighbours to keep an eye on them, she worries about them all the time. She takes her oldest daughter with her to her place of work, ostensibly to help with her tasks but really because Ruksana feels that she, at the age of 14, is more vulnerable than the younger two. She is coming close to marriageable age and Ruksana does not want to jeopardise her chances of making a good match by leaving her exposed to the risk of becoming a victim of unpoliced male desire. She believes that the younger girls are safer – a dangerous calculation, but indispensable for the sake of earning a living and to calm her own unquiet mind. Ruksana's husband died three years ago. He was a rickshaw driver. When he became sick with diabetes, he could not afford to take time from work to recover and had no money for medicine. He died pedalling his rickshaw.

Male unemployment is conspicuous. Young men, obviously without occupation, lounge, lean and wait, full of unwanted energy and unused power. They play cricket on rubble-strewn waste ground, share a cigarette, hang on each other's shoulders, wrestle and fight. The time between puberty and marriage is a prolonged adolescence, inactive, time unfilled, longing unfulfilled. This is fertile terrain for disaffection and recruitment to gangs. It is not reasonable to expect those in their prime to wait meekly for a fate foretold; they are bound to find some activity that claims their fidgety spirit and discarded vigour. I came across one group of boys, aged about 16 or 17, standing in shadow so that the images would show up more clearly, showing each other hardcore pornography they had downloaded onto their mobile phone: scenes of unerotic sex, 'blue movies', with Western actors, at which they laughed and simulated uneasy arousal, perhaps to conceal the frustration of repressed desire: none of this alien iconography is calculated to inspire in them respect for women, a failing with which non-Muslims frequently taunt them. Most older men work – as masons, rickshaw drivers, daily labourers, van-pullers, electricians and roof-tilers. But many of these are also underoccupied, working at a level below their skill; and in any case, many regard their often-slender income as their own property, to spend as they choose.

## VII
## LIVES OF ADDICTION

Topsia is known in the wider city as a place where drugs may be acquired cheaply and consumed with impunity; a 'safe' place, where people go unchallenged by an authority which profits from their addiction. This neglect incurs great risks. It is not that the victims are going to rise up against those who devastate their lives. The danger comes from those more articulate and educated, moved by the revulsion this inspires in them, who may become 'radicalised', inspired to act not simply on behalf of their co-religionists but of their fellow human-beings. This is, after all, the way that most radical or revolutionary movements grow: driven by intellectuals, theorists and the educated disaffected, people often at a remove from those in whose name they act and whom they enlist as ghost armies against oppression, with or without their consent.

Certainly, the neglect of the unpersons of Topsia suggests a high degree of cynicism and connivance by elements of the State. It is impossible to remain indifferent to this highly visible spectacle of institutionalised self-harm; which is, perhaps, why it remains 'unknown' to those in power, a blank space, not only on city maps but also in the mind of the rulers of Kolkata and West Bengal.

I met Mohammad Shahzade, a wasted young man of 26, who lives in Auddybegan, a former Anglo–Indian settlement on the edge of Tiljala. He works pulling a van, a cart attached to a cycle for the transport of goods. He can earn between 200 and 250 rupees a day. He is married with one little girl of four. The family lives in a single room. His mother came from Mumbai after the death of his father, perhaps in flight from grief. Mohammad Shahzade scarcely knows how he became addicted. He watched his friends, and when they offered to share the pleasure of drugs with him, he did not refuse. He inhales Dendrite adhesive, a viscous yellow substance normally used to attach uppers to the soles of footwear. Mohammad Shahzade squeezes about half the contents of the tube into a transparent plastic bag. He bunches the bag around his nose and mouth and draws a deep breath. As he exhales, his breath silvers the inside of the bag; several times his sharp intake of air collapses the bag and then fills it out again. He adds some more of the 'solution' to intensify the high. He looks up, his eyes wounded, a despairing vacancy. His speech is slurred. When he tries to explain the satisfaction he gets from the drug, he says, 'There is a magnetism in the brain. You feel you are no longer confined, but you are outside yourself, no longer restricted by your own life.' Each blue-and-yellow tube of the adhesive costs twelve rupees. Mohammad Shahadze uses five or six tubes a day – 60 or 70 rupees, money that he knows he should spend on his family. He does not work every day. Sometimes he is not fit to do so. At such times, he borrows money from his wife's parents. He suffers chest pains. There is occasionally blood in his urine.

Mohammad Shahzade also takes brown sugar (heroin). This gives a different sensation altogether. It arouses him sexually. He says he desperately wants to give up. His wife pleads with him *'Chor do'* (leave it, please leave it), but he cannot. He says, 'If you admit me to a rehabilitation centre

I'll be able to conquer it, but I cannot do it on my own. My wife will come with me. I feel shame and sadness. There is no one to help me.'

As we walk through the long desolate thoroughfare of the island, a number of young men, many also with an air of impaired consciousness, plead for help; most ask for money, which, they say, they will use to gain release from their addiction. It is a wretched scene: emaciated young men, gaunt and ravaged when they should be full of life and energy, emblems of dependency, of which drugs are a powerful metaphor. Indeed, drugs occupy a sensitive place in the market economy, for they demonstrate the theory of supply and demand in its purest, almost abstract, form. Nobody actually demanded it until it became available: the supply engenders its own addictive loyalty. It is the supreme market relationship. This is why whenever drugs are intercepted by officials their street value is announced, because this exempts the market from the taint of illicit goods.

Mohammad Shamim's experience is very different. He is originally from Kidderpore, a long-established less-wretched Muslim area, but now lives with his wife close to Topsia. He is well dressed, in smart blue jeans and a yellow shirt. Apparently sincere and talkative, he speaks with a frankness born perhaps of the substances he has taken. He has been dependent on drugs for a long time. He married a year and a half ago but discovered drugs long before, when he was playing football. He joined a club, and someone told him he would enhance his performance by taking brown sugar. Mohammad Shamim wants to prove that he is in control of his life. He heard of a Brazilian football player who, after taking drugs, fell down on the football field and died. This is a deterrent. 'I take drugs in a limited manner. I use alcohol, but never on Thursday or Fridays' (this apparently for religious reasons). 'On those days I don't take Bagpiper (whisky), only beer.' He says this as though in expectation of praise for his capacity for renunciation.

Mohammad Shamim is an electrician, a trade taught him by his father. He prefers to work alone, since by doing so he can keep more of his income as it is not monitored by his family. His father has taken him all over India, in an effort to break his drug habit. They have been to rehabilitation and detoxification centres in Mumbai and Delhi:

> He even started the business for me, to get me out of drugs. One thing I have learned is that in this business, your friends are your best enemies. Since marriage, I tried to stay away from drugs, but I can't. I have already spent 350 rupees (about $8) this morning, and the evening is still to come.

Suddenly, Mohammad Shamim dropped his bravado. His lips trembled and a perfect teardrop formed on his lower eyelid. 'I am thinking what will happen to me in the future. I do not want my mother to know how badly affected I am. She is always begging me to stop and I tell her I will. I expect she has called me this morning.' He looks at me with beseeching eyes, a look of helpless contrition.

Mohammad Shamim takes a mobile phone out of his jeans pocket and checks his calls. He confirms there has indeed been a call from his mother and asks to be excused while he talks to her. As he speaks, he cries, and tears spill down his cheek. 'Sorry Mummy', he says. 'I will try. I don't want to hurt you. Ask the doctor.' He closes his mobile, crying softly. Unfortunately for him, he had left the phone on loudspeaker, and both the tone and the age of the voice made it plain that he was not talking to his mother at all. The levity of the woman's tone was plainly audible. It emerged that he has a lot of girl-friends – some who subsidise his addiction – and it was to one of these he had been speaking, in the hope of softening my heart and opening up my wallet.

Unaware that he has openly demonstrated his manipulative powers, he continued to talk of his efforts towards rehabilitation. 'I was admitted to detoxification units, but it was always possible to find people there who would help us get drugs, so it was no use.' Mohammad Shamim proved also to be a somewhat vainglorious young man of 23. He boasted that he has also been an 'anti-social'. He has been something of a desperado, and the police demanded a proportion of the proceeds of his crimes. 'I have already committed murder', he says, 'although the victim didn't actually die. I shot him in the stomach, but the bullet went into his thigh. He was a high-ranking person; I was jailed, but the next day I was released, because I have the blessing of an important politician. When the police caught me, they asked me to work for them.'

Mohammad Shamim's wife is pregnant. That is why he wants to give up drugs, he says.

I tried after marriage, but could not. If I am asked which I prefer, my wife or drugs, I will say my wife; but the drugs have greater power over me. All my family are angry with me. I feel ashamed of what I have done with my life. My father and sister have both spent so much money, but it has not worked. I used to take drugs in the bathroom of my sister's home. When my brother-in-law found out he fought with me, because he wanted to prevent me from ruining my life.

I have asked my mother to give me more time. If I cannot break it, I will go for a religious life, since it is *haram* [forbidden] in our faith ... I'll give up brown sugar ... But when I am heartbroken I only take alcohol.

Mohammad Shamim lingered after our conversation, to discover whether or not he had moved me and if so, how much I would give him. Mohammad Shamim was accompanied by a young boy, Mohammad Sono, who said he was 18 but looked far younger. He had the large hands and feet of an adolescent, a hairless face and a slightly stupefied expression, which reminded me of photographs of late Victorian schoolchildren – faces puffy with malnutrition, excessive carbohydrate and lack of vitamins. Mohammad Sono's face was disfigured by boils, his hair crinkled away from a broad forehead. He was even dressed in the same colours as Mohammad Shamim, who is apparently a model and inspiration to him. He lives in Park Circus, a chaotic community of slums, tenements and pavement dwellings. He has been brought up by his mother and two sisters. His father re-married and ran away, and Mohammad Sono has no memory of him. His addiction started 'six or seven years ago'. As a street child, he had started smoking 'ganja' with friends.

As Mohammad Sono is talking, Ali, our friend and companion, a social worker, says that he once spent a night in jail in the same cell as this boy. Ali had been victim of a false charge brought against him (a common experience, especially when disputed property is involved). He had been incarcerated with Mohammad Sono, picked up on the streets the same day. He can vouch for the truth of what Mohammad Sono says. Quite simply, he complains that if he does not get the drugs he needs he feels pain – in his legs, his arms, his whole body. To feed his addiction, he says, 'I steal anything. I can't help it. Without drugs my whole body aches, I cannot sleep, I cannot stay still.' On his restless progress through the city each day, Mohammad Sono has developed a sixth sense of what can be taken without being caught: any unsupervised goods, any

apparent piece of waste material with a market value, any
unguarded thing that can be quickly exchanged for cash – he
has developed an almost supernatural speed in appropriating
and selling it. He has an acute sense of the market for stolen
goods; an ingenuity that in other circumstances might make
him an accomplished player in the more formal economy.
Today, he came to Topsia with 400 rupees ($9), of which
200 remain in his pocket.

His special expertise lies in stealing from construction sites.
He steals iron rods used for reinforcing concrete, pieces of
iron, steel. He walks calmly onto the site, picks up whatever
he knows he can sell, and walks out with it. Today he stole
a piece of iron. He takes it to the recycling unit, where he
can get five to ten rupees per kilo. Aluminium is the most
valuable metal, worth ten times as much as iron. Of course,
he is regularly caught by the police. He spends a night or two
in jail and is then released, since his incarceration serves no
purpose. His mother has no idea of the life he leads, but he
is so caught up in it that for him nothing exists outside a life
of perpetually renewed highs and the ingenuity of procuring
the means to sustain it.

It was difficult to separate the stories we were told from
the fictions spun by the heightened states of mind of those we
spoke with. Sheikh Badal, a much older man with grizzled
hair, wearing a blue check lungi, said, gesturing to the drugs,
'My life is lost in this.' Earlier, he used to drink country-made
liquor. His mother migrated with him, his brother and two
sisters from the Sunderbans when he was a child. His father
did not come with them, and his mother told the children
he had died. In the city, one of his sisters died. His mother
worked as a maidservant to keep the family together, and they
lived in a rented hut by the canalside. Sheikh Badal drove

a rickshaw for 20 years. His wife is working as a domestic servant, his two daughters are married and his two sons are both working in a small shoemaking unit.

Sheikh Badal says that drinking chulai was cheap, and cost only ten to 15 rupees a day. Eight years ago, he started taking hard drugs and, weakened as a result, his earnings as a rickshaw driver have fallen to 60–70 rupees a day (about $1.30) once he has paid the 50 rupees to the owner of the vehicle. 'The drug', he says, 'is everywhere. You cannot escape it. If I do not take it, I have abdominal pain, vomiting, I cannot work. I would like to go for rehabilitation, but it costs 1500 rupees for a ten-day period [$30].' How does he get money for drugs? 'Sometimes', he says, 'I find a piece of iron I can sell, I find it easier to collect scrap metal than to drive a rickshaw. If I have nothing, I beg money from my son. How can he refuse me?'

When he gets drugs, he shares them with friends; on days when he has none, he curls up and sleeps. His family threw him out of the house. He was told he had to give up drugs or sleep on the pavement. Sheikh Badal believes that the advantage of living here is that people understand what it means to be addicted. He sometimes begs, and if he knocks on doors, people give him leftovers. He feels shame, but if he takes drugs he has no sense of hunger:

> My wife says she will take me back if I give up, but where will I get the money to be rehabilitated? I am spending 50 rupees twice a day for one pellet of brown sugar. Sometimes I steal. I was arrested for theft and spent 28 days in jail. The police know about Topsia, but they won't come because they take money from the dealers.

Later that afternoon, I saw Sheikh Badal again. He, too, was dealing. When he saw me, he quickly disappeared. A little after that, a commotion arose at one of the entrances to the settlement, and there was an unusual flurry of activity. This soon subsided. It was caused by the appearance of what might, ironically, be called 'police informers.' Two men in plain clothes, certainly police, had come to inform the drug dealers that they might expect a raid later in the day. These members of the police force are in the pay of the dealers, and they come to make sure that those who bribe them will not be found with large quantities of either drugs or cash. The law operates here, if at all, in slow motion and, for a price, can be prevented from functioning at all.

The addicts of Topsia have no need to disguise their condition. A striking young man of 18, Mohammad Shamim admits to spending between 600 and 700 rupees a day on drugs ($15), a sum far beyond the income of any workman. He has been addicted for four years. His father has a furniture workshop in another part of Topsia. He is, he says disarmingly, a 'lifter', who picks pockets in the bus or the Kolkata Metro. This is an art that has to be acquired and his teacher, he says, was the necessity for drugs. He goes out armed because he knows that if he is caught by passengers on the bus or metro, he will be beaten, even to death. He has a blade with which he threatens them and usually they leave him with their wallet. If they still try to retrieve it, he will attack. Shamim studied in a government school to Class V, until he was eleven. Then he made friends 'with the wrong people'. His brother works in his father's workshop and so, in theory, does Shamim. He takes his father's bicycle to fetch wood and materials for the workshop, but in his excursions through the city he often stops off at Topsia. He thinks his family knows nothing of his way of life. Whenever he has been arrested and jailed, he tells them he has been to Mumbai for a trip. Sometimes he would like to give up drugs, but life is exciting, and once you have known the high, you want to recapture it all the time; the world of work and family becomes dull and predictable.

The most poignant drug story from Topsia proved to be a fabrication, although even the fanciful tale was less dramatic than the truth. Mitoon is a slight young man of 22, with straight hair parted in the middle. He wears a black vest bordered with red, dusty knee-length jeans and rubber flip-flops. One arm is severed just below the shoulder and the other at the elbow. He is accompanied by a much younger boy, Ravi, who is about 13. Ravi wears a dingy-yellow knitted hat on top of his curly hair, and a shirt and jeans; he also wears a look of professional vulnerability which, it turns out, is useful to his calling. Mitoon and Ravi are brothers. They are inseparable, and Mitoon is dependent on the younger boy. Mitoon lost his limbs as the result of an accident when he was ten. Their parents had died and, at that time, he used to work as a vendor of cold drinks in the train. He had gone to fetch two buckets of water to mix with the lemon to make *nimbu pani* (lemonade) when he stumbled and was knocked over by a train close to Park Circus station. He was run over by the train and passed out. Nobody took him to hospital, no one came to attend to his injuries. After a time, he regained consciousness and walked to the hospital. The wounds to his arms became infected and both had to be amputated. The boys sleep on the pavement or under any verandah or shelter they can find. They earn a living by Ravi's singing in the bus. 'People see my disability, and when they hear him sing, they give money.' Ravi sings a hymn – in English – that he learned from a period of 'rehabilitation' (a widely-used term, and of interest since it suggests some kind of restoration to a former state that most of its objects have never enjoyed) with the Genesis Foundation. He accompanies himself with two flat stones held between his first and second fingers, by means of which he maintains a rhythmic beat. He has a plaintive voice, and although the words are not clear they tell of Joy to the World because the Lord is Born. Ravi is addicted to brown sugar, while Mitoon has been a user for several years. Ravi says their father and mother died in a road accident. His mother had been an air hostess. They were born in a village in the North 24 Parganas district of Bengal, and came with their parents to Kolkata as small children. They do not know hunger because brown sugar takes away the appetite. If they do not take drugs, they vomit, suffer severe stomach pain and their ears suppurate. They say they are devoted to one another, understand each other's feelings, and share every pain and sorrow. Mitoon cannot quit. It is the dealers who should be punished, he says virtuously; but the political parties, the local mafia and police are all involved.

This account was far from true. Mitoon, it appeared, according to those who had known him, was actually an accomplished pickpocket, a trade he had followed since an early addiction to brown sugar. When robbing someone in a train he was caught, and attacked by an angry mob. The injuries he received to his hands and arms did indeed become infected, and this is why they were amputated. The boys are not brothers and they are not orphans. Their parents live in Dhapapada, a settlement that makes a livelihood out of the Kolkata municipal tip, where they work as ragpickers. Mitoon and Ravi actually sleep in the huts where drugs are consumed; whether their parents are aware of the activities of their boys is not known. They do indeed sing and beg in the train, despite the drastic aversion therapy Mitoon might have been expected to receive from operating on the railways. They work out of Howrah Station: Mitoon needs someone talented, since he cannot earn alone. He exercises a visible power over the younger boy. Ravi sings, while Mitoon displays his disability. But they do not operate alone. They are in a team of pickpockets who, while the listeners are entranced by the winsome adolescent, divest their victims of their valuables. Mitoon has been at least three times to rehabilitation centres, but returns to the only realistic way he has of making some kind of livelihood.

They change their names frequently – sometimes Hindu, sometimes Muslim. There is another invisible player in their sad theatrics – the stories they invent are inspired by TV soap opera and serials, which abound in tales of orphans, car and plane crashes, the glamour of the life of air hostesses and the tragic destiny of the forsaken. Commercial culture also prompts the plot-lines and colours the stories that procure them a livelihood. The convergence of powerful social forces propels them to a life likely to be as brief as it is violent. We offered to buy them a good meal. They were not hungry, they insisted. When they saw our generosity was likely to be withdrawn, they changed their mind. They ate a biryani at a roadside *dhaba* with every sign of enjoyment.


## VIII
## COMPASSION


If these communities have not been entirely abandoned, this is not because of any effort by government or other state agencies. Mercy and compassion are strictly a result of voluntary effort, sometimes organised by non-government agencies, but even more effectively by those – often motivated by a sense of religion – who regard it as their duty to serve the most outcast. Jabeen has worked with the families of the children who attend the small non-government organisation school, children who largely melted away with the discontinuance of the midday meal. She passes unmolested each day through scenes of despair, since it is known that it is not her purpose to betray the people to authority – an authority not simply indifferent to their sufferings but also only too eager to profit from them. Jabeen says that the fire that removed people from the opposite bank of the canal was deliberately lit. Fire is one of the principal social cleansing agents used by those in power to get rid of unwanted squatters. The city council intended to widen a road, so it ordered the people to move. When they refused to do so, political arson determined their fate; particularly since a majority were supporters of the opposition Trinamool Congress.

> Most people in Topsia worked in the tanneries. As polluting industries, these were closed down and removed outside the city limits. All permanent staff went with them. Casual workers remained, and men took up driving rickshaws, while women became maidservants, or worked trimming the straps of chappals. There are about 750 families here, that is, about 5,000 people. Some stay only part-time, returning to their village to work as sharecroppers or casual labourers on other people's land. There they will have a hut of mud and wood. Many of the men have come from Bihar and have married Bengali girls. They are no longer really country people, but neither are they of the city.

Jabeen was herself to learn the meaning of compassion from the people to whom she has been committed. In April 2010 she fell sick. She was admitted to hospital where a hysterectomy was performed. When they learned that she was dangerously ill, the poor people of Topsia, the most impoverished of Kolkata, made a collection of money for her. They brought it to the nursing home. Jabeen told them they should keep it, and she would let them know if it were needed. Among the donations was a gift of 5000 rupees from one of the drug-dealers – the very people Jabeen is trying to put out of business. Every day, so many visitors from Topsia came, that the staff in the nursing-home wondered why she had so many friends, and why they were all so poor.

In May 2010 I went to see Jabeen, who was at her mother's house in a small compound in Beckbagan, also a Muslim community in central Kolkata. This house was constructed by Jabeen's maternal grandfather on ancestral land – a small courtyard opening onto four or five rooms. The household consists of Jabeen's mother, two of her sons, their wives and one child. Jabeen's uncle also stays there: he is deaf and dumb, a small animated man, now retired, who used to make a living by drawing posters for films. To pay for Jabeen's treatment, her daughter took a loan of 35,000 rupees. Jabeen has been much moved by the loyalty of the people towards her. She is kept informed of everything that happens in Topsia while she has been ill. Her eyes and ears are everywhere in the community. She says, 'The love of the people has done more to restore me to health than any medicine.'


## IX
## RESISTING DRUG CULTURE

I asked Jabeen about the effect of this poisonous culture on those who are not part of it, people who have been driven by misfortune or chance to this most derelict of sites. Rashida

Begum had already provided some insight into the fears many parents and grandparents entertain for a generation growing up in this environment of social, as well as material, pollution. She is far from alone. Jabeen introduced us to Hamida Begum.

Hamida Begum has five children. Her husband is a mason and electrician, but work is irregular, and in any case he gives her only 30 or 40 rupees from his daily earnings of about 100 rupees ($2) as the rest is spent on chulai. Hamida works cutting rubber from the uppers of chappals. She is paid one rupee per dozen, and if she works all day she can earn between 30 and 40 rupees. Her children attend school. Her mother came originally from Bihar, like a majority of the Urdu-speaking Muslims in the poorest parts of Kolkata. Since her mother died they have no remaining link with Bihar. Hamida's eldest boy works as a ragpicker. He is twelve. He also has tuberculosis.

When Hamida Begum tells her story, she speaks of her individual fate, although in fact, she is part of a great collective migration that created an enclave of Urdu-speaking Muslim culture in the heart of the capital of West Bengal:

> My sister was living here with her husband and she suggested that we should join her, since with irregular income and a growing family we could not afford to stay in Rajabazar where my mother lived. This is an unsafe place. We were living on the other side of the canal, but our hut was burned down. Drug addicts come and steal from us. One of my children became addicted, but now he has left it. He is still only 13. Can you imagine, small children become addicted? I sent him to my brother's place, so that he should be away from here. I think only of getting out of this place, but without money, I have no option.

Hamida Begum is a thin woman full of unquiet energy. She wears a dark red saree, cheap chappals and silver earrings.

The bangles on her skinny wrist clash, a metallic music, each time she moves her arm.

> We pay only 200 rupees in rent. My daughter works with me cutting rubber for the factories in Shivtala. She collects the work from the factory and returns it at the end of the day. There are several hundred women and girls doing this work here. It is easy, even young children can do it. I have one boy who is rag-picking. Some days he comes home with 30 or 40 rupees, sometimes nothing. It is dirty and dangerous work. You can understand why even children want to take drugs. It looks to them like an escape from here. But it only leads them into a different kind of prison.
>
> Together we usually manage to make 100 rupees a day, but if we are sick or have nothing, I beg. Sometimes I borrow from the grocery shop, and pay back after two or three days. I buy one and a half kilos of rice for 25 rupees. I have a ration card from Rajabazar, but I cannot use it here. Firewood costs five rupees a kilo. Potatoes had become expensive, but now the price has come down again. If we live to see another day, it is by the grace of Allah.

## X
### FEAR FOR THE YOUNG

Along the length of the canalside, a frieze of anxious women with similar tales, mothers the only shield their children have against the temptation of drugs. Sahari Begum has lived here five years. She has three children aged nine, five and four. Her husband was a brass worker, but his skill became redundant because no one is buying brass vessels any more. He now works as a daily wage labourer wherever he can, and earns 50–60 rupees a day ($1.25). He is a victim of a wider de-skilling of Muslims in India. Globalisation has eroded artisanal crafts, as industrial goods displace traditional handicrafts. A disproportionate number of those whose livelihood has been degraded are Muslim, including workers in woodcarving, pottery, silk-weaving, embroidery and *chikan*-work, hand-made carpets, brass and metal work, tanning, leather and lock-making. Imported goods, industrially made objects, erase old skills in the twinkling of an eye without providing an alternative. In any case, the percentage of Muslims in regular employment, in both the public and private sectors, has been in decline ever since Independence.[6]

'We were living in Mullickpur, but could not pay the rent,' says Sahari Begum, gesturing to her present home;

> Here we are simply passing our days. I have to stay. Where will we find the money to go elsewhere? I am afraid for my children's future. There is no law here. Sometimes, the police raid, but who will they catch? The drug-dealers all run away, because they get a tip-off from the police.

Sahari Begum cooks snacks – *papad* and *alu bara* – which she sells by the side of her hut. For every 100 rupees invested, she makes a profit of 25–30. She sits at the small table for between four and five hours a day. She has a stove fuelled with wood in a little depression in the earth, on which stands a heavy metal skillet that is half-filled with transparent bubbling oil; into this she dips the papad and deep-fries the potato snacks. It is becoming harder to find customers, since with the rising price of oil and fuel, the papad she used to sell at one rupee a piece is now one and a half rupees.

Yasmin Begum used to work in a godown [warehouse] re-cycling plastic for 80 rupees a day, but she gave it up, forfeiting vital income, to watch over her children who are at risk from the lure of the drug-dealers – the main power in the community. They are not the majority, she insists, but they have the contacts and the money:

> Even though they are shunned by those who want their children to grow up to be good honest citizens, their eyes are on them, because it is through them that their future profit is assured. They often give a free sample of brown sugar to get the young men hooked.

Yasmin Begum has lived in Topsia for a year. She married ten years ago, and her husband worked in a leather factory. One day, while trying to adjust some electrical fitting, he fell from the ladder and injured his ribs. Since that time, he has been unable to do heavy labour and is now occupied gluing the soles of shoes to the uppers for 400 rupees a week. Yasmin Begum needs at least 100 rupees a day to feed the family, but with the rent for the hut costing 400 rupees a month she rarely has enough to satisfy their hunger. She takes goods on credit at the grocery store, but has to repay within a few days or the supply will cease. Yasmin Begum studied only until she was ten, but she wants to educate her own children so that they will escape the destiny that lies in wait for them in this poisonous locality.

Many of the women who are so vigilant for their children are unable to read or write, but they show a fierce resolve to defend those they love. The women of Topsia offer rich instruction in the difference between the truly intelligent and the merely educated. It is impossible to overstate the perceptiveness and insight of unlettered women, in moral and social questions – a knowledge often effaced in those transformed by the sometimes ambiguous benefits of schooling.

Masuda Bibi sits on the threshold of her hut, one panel of which evidently belonged to a bag of something called sodium formate, lamenting that she must live among so much 'social pollution'. 'Our children cannot have a future as human beings while they are brought up here.' Masuda, from Joynagar in South 24 Parganas, has lived in Kolkata for ten years. She came to join her parents, who lived as encroachers on the road. She tells how Javed Khan brought them here. He was, until May 2010, the local councilor for Topsia, and it was a name we were to hear frequently. Because this ward was one reserved for women in the Kolkata municipal election, Javed Khan was moved to an adjacent area. He lost the seat, but his wife now represents the people of Topsia. Javed Khan is spoken of as a benefactor, but some women observed that it is a strange kind of philanthropy that brings children into such an atmosphere. Masuda Bibi says he had the huts built following the fire that destroyed the community on the other side of the canal, and this may account for the uniformity in the size of the dwellings. Masuda Bibi's husband is a rickshaw puller. They have four daughters, and the eldest is already working as a rubber-cutter in making chappals.

After considerable efforts to contact him, we had a brief conversation with Javed Khan. His account of the sufferings of the people of Topsia distributed blame between the long rule of the Communist Party of India (Marxist) (CPI[M]) and the people themselves. He said the ruling party has used Muslims only as a vote-bank, and it was part of their plan to keep them 'financially weak' and separate from society. Although he says he is doing his best to assure their well-being, they are also to be blamed for their abjection.

We need to raise ourselves, but few efforts are made. Most people do not send their children to school, and those who do drop out. Only education can change the fate of Muslims. We are planning to launch an awareness programme in Muslim areas, where we will ask parents to send their children to school, rather than send them to work in hotels and factories.

He had little sympathy for the people along the canal, which he says have become the haunts of anti-socials. The police know about the drug business, but they are hand in glove with the dealers and get commission from them. As a diagnosis of the ills of poor Muslim communities in Kolkata, this was both banal and barely distinguishable from the words of the CPI(M). The easy advocacy of 'educational awareness' omits the most obvious element – the disenchantment of generations of young men in particular, who have been educated and still remain without employment. We were to hear much more on this theme.

I met the Imam of the mosque, which is at the far end of the island, close to the East Metropolitan By-Pass. It is one of the few brick buildings, washed pale green. On the walls are red-painted images, clearly executed by loving amateurs – a Holy Book, flowers and candles, a red dome and a minaret. The Imam is an unremarkable-looking man in late middle age, wearing a blue lungi and chappals, bare-chested, not easily distinguishable from the people he serves and among whom he lives. I asked him whether poverty made people less observant of religion. He said that being poor sets people apart from society, and although poverty did not affect religious belief, becoming involved in drugs and crime certainly did. 'Our people will never lose their faith, because they know that many have followed their religion even at the cost of their life. It may be that they do not say *namaz* [prayers] or come to the mosque, but that does not mean the spark is not there, that their conscience has died. When conscience dies, the human being dies also. They may not practise their religion, but one day the spark will be kindled and they will return.'

The huts stand open to the narrow thoroughfare, so that it is impossible to keep secrets of any kind: a man is separating the plastic from the metal needle of syringes in a pile of medical waste on the floor of his hut. A child, no more than a year old, plays with an outsized pair of scissors that lie in the bowl from where its mother is paring rubber thongs for chappals: even the baby's play foreshadows the joyless labour she can expect in her life. A hawker sells vegetables which have been grown on the toxic wastes of the municipal dump. Along the pathway shuffles, in slow procession, the drug-wounded, casualties of the war of the rich against the poor, eyes unfocussed, walking unsteadily, elderly men, fathers of families, boys who have only just reached adolescence. Some hold out their hands in entreaty, begging for money that will certainly find its way into the palms of the dealers.

## XI
## MIGRATIONS

Although for many of the families in Topsia, memories of migration from Bihar are faint, and a sense of their rural origins has long lapsed, they remain Biharis.

Since British times there has been continuous migration from Bihar, and this did not cease with Independence. Hindu and Muslim migrants came to Kolkata, both as lone men to work as labourers in the docks, as rickshaw pullers and in construction, and as whole families of the landless. Urdu-speaking Muslims increasingly settled where they could maintain their language and culture, and today these form the distinctive inner-city settlements of the city. Although many also know Bengali, they persist in a tradition distinct from that of Bengali Muslims, whose religious sensibility is inflected by an ancient, syncretic Bengali culture, in which Allah co-existed with older deities, at whose shrines both Hindus and Muslims offered boughs of scarlet hibiscus and garlands of sweet jasmine.

There is a curious parallel between the isolation of these Muslims and the 1.25 million or so Biharis who chose to go to East Pakistan in the 1960s. This was partly a belated response to Partition, and a result of communal disturbances in Bihar. The exodus was undertaken in the conviction that opportunities for advancement for Muslims would be greater in Pakistan than in India. These unfortunates were overtaken by the Bangladeshi liberation war of 1971, when they sided with Pakistan. They were reviled and stigmatised by Bengalis, labelled as collaborators and forced to take refuge in urban refugee camps, protected by the United Nations. Many camps – notably Geneva Camp in Mohammadpur, Dhaka – subsequently became city settlements remarkably similar to those in Kolkata. In Kolkata, Muslims found themselves in territory hostile to them for different reasons. Most Muslims in West Bengal are Bengali-speaking and, for the past third of a century, West Bengal has been governed by the CPI(M). Many Bengali Muslims have certainly been beneficiaries of the CPI(M), since land reform permitted many to rise from the insecurity of landlessness and sharecropping to become small landowners. But the city was for many years neglected by the CPI(M), and with it the Urdu-speaking Muslim poor, who have become alienated both from the Marxist rhetoric of the CPI(M) and from the capitalist reality of their policy in the past decade. It is a historic irony that Bihari Muslims, some of whom fled to East Pakistan and some of whom sought a better livelihood in Kolkata, should both, in their way, have been stranded, so that there has been a clear convergence in their fate of isolation, with their lives apart from the mainstream. While many younger Biharis in Bangladesh have grown up to be Bengali-speakers, no longer distinguishable from the majority, this is less true of Kolkata's Urdu-speakers: Dhaka's Biharis are more easily absorbed, because there is no religious divide.

In Topsia we came across a strange phenomenon, although not uncommon in Kolkata: Munni Bibi came with her parents as a child from a village in the south of West Bengal. She has lived most of her life in Topsia and, over the years, stopped speaking Bengali and learned to express herself in Urdu – a curious adaptation of someone from the dominant Bengali culture adjusting to the circumstances of the narrower world of Urdu, which, in Kolkata, is associated with poverty and reduced life-chances.

When we met Munni Bibi, she had other things to think about than cultural modification: her house had been blown down in the pre-monsoon storms of early May. It stood, a wrecked tangle of bamboo, wood and twisted metal, destroyed by a single gust of wind. She and her husband, and their five children have been sleeping in the school for the past few weeks. Munni Bibi's husband is a cart-puller; he is, she says, a good husband who brings home all of the money that he earns – between 100 and 150 rupees a day ($2–3). This provides half of what would be necessary to feed a family of seven adequately. Munni Bibi has no chance of finding the money required to rebuild her ruined home. Where will they go, the rejected of rural life, the unwanted of the city?

## XII
## THE MAIN ROAD

The wooden bridge that joins the island to the main road
has almost collapsed under the weight of the motorcycles
that have been driven across it, and it sags dangerously on
one side towards the greenish water. Wooden barriers have
been placed at either end, so that people must climb over
or bend beneath them if they want to reach the island. The
bridge was damaged in September 2009. Nine months later,
no effort had been made to repair it.

The main road is flanked on one side by huts, small waste
recycling units and larger scale enterprises where plastic is
sorted. Some are highly specialised. One deals exclusively
with silver paper: the sun plays on crinkled silver, tinsel, foil
and wrappings, so that the heaps of waste sparkle like an
extensive hoard of treasure. On the opposite side of the road,
a construction site displays a board with an artist's impression
of the 20-storey towers to be built there: gleaming white
and separated by emerald-coloured turf. The building is to
be called Lakeside, although the only water in sight is the
stinking foam of the canal, and even this less-than-pastoral
vista is obscured by the poor hovels of Topsia. It is difficult
to imagine that the future inhabitants of this luxury condo
will want to gaze out at the misery in front of their new
dwellings; so even if the people living on the sidewalk are
not displaced by the actual construction, this will certainly be
their fate once the high-rise is established. This colonisation
of the city space is conspicuous, and it is not ashamed to call
itself by its name: on more than one name-plate in the private
palaces of India's cities, I have seen the title 'Colonizer and
Developer'; and, indeed, many upper-income communities

call themselves, in an ironic parody of the vision of their former masters, 'colonies'.


## XIII
### AN INJURED WOMAN

Outside one rough wooden dwelling we catch a glimpse of a young woman, who tries, with the edge of her saree, to conceal two wounds on her face and neck. She disappears quickly into one of the dark interiors. Someone explains laconically that her husband had cut her with a knife because he suspected her of an extra-marital affair.

A few days later, we were able to speak with her. There was an angry scar on her cheek and her lower arm was still bandaged. She is Moina, and her husband fled after he had assaulted her. She is still suffering from shock and embarrassment, and her mother, Manwara, takes over the story.

Manwara is an extremely handsome woman in her fifties, whose good looks are emphasised by the absence of ornaments: there is the trace of a flower where a nose-stud once was, and the mark of rings in her ears. She wears an orange blouse and dark red saree. Despite the lines on her face, her eyes are animated and expressive. She says that 'some local people' had told Moina's husband that she was seeing another man. In his rage he attacked her, and then, overcome by remorse at what he had done, ran away. The police are looking for him, she said, although without any great urgency. He had tried to cut his wife's throat, but as she raised her hand to defend herself, the knife had slashed only her cheek and wrist.

Manwara was born in Topsia. She lived on the site of what is now the East Metropolitan Bypass and came here when they were evicted. She raised her children by begging. Eventually she bought a van – a cycle cart for carrying goods – which she rented out daily, but two years ago it was stolen,

> Now I have nothing. In 1964 I saw the riots between Hindus and Muslims. I was a child, and we hid inside the mosque. I was born in the Sunderbans, where most of our family lived and died. My mother came to Kolkata when my father abandoned her.

Manwara was married at 15 to an older man. At 18 she was a widow:

> He was a drinker who took all kinds of poisonous liquor. It ruined his stomach and killed him. He used to sell cinema tickets on the black market, and was already over 40 when we married. I have spent most of my life as a widow.

Manwara says she is 'no longer in touch' with her older daughter. This is obviously some kind of metaphor, for the next time we saw her she was in a group of women including her other daughter. She said that they no longer share a kitchen, a symbolic estrangement that Manwara felt was self-explanatory. Manwara could have married a second time, but she would not. Her sister had married for a second time and her husband insisted that she leave her children. This, Manwara was unwilling to risk, so she decided to remain independent. She taught herself the skills necessary for survival, especially embroidery which she also taught in a workshop for many years.

Manwara regrets that Moina, like herself, married young. Moina was married at 14. The marriage was a necessity, because she had been seen talking to the man who then became her husband. After the attack on her, she wants a divorce, 'but where will people like us find the money to pay a lawyer?' Manwara says all her relatives are now 'above', which she indicates with a raised eyebrow. She speaks as though they were simply in an adjacent room; and perhaps that is how she feels, since the passage between life and death is casual and frequent in these sites of affliction. Manwara calls to her grandson, a little boy of about six. She raises his T-shirt and shows the scar of an operation across his stomach. He was born with a deformity that prevented him from passing water. He has undergone two operations on his bladder, but needs medicine that costs 50 rupees a day, which is as much as Moina's husband earns; and that income has now fled with him. Manwara has pawned all her jewellery, her nose-studs and earrings, so that they can eat and the little boy can receive the medicine he needs to survive; but even that money is running out.

Three months later, I met Manwara again. She looked thinner and more haggard. She was working, sorting waste materials in a godown run by Tiljala-SHED. Her daughter, Moina, has left home and 'married' again. She has taken her child, and Manwara is now living alone. Moina never even calls. This is a very recent indicator of abandonment in the families of slumdwellers. People have regularly disappeared, proved untraceable; but the mobile phone has been an instrument of connection between even the poorest people, and Manwara's complaint against her daughter is both as old as humanity and extremely contemporary. Manwara is also drinking because of loneliness. She laments that she has brought up her children without male support and harmed no one. Recently she went to hospital, where the doctor diagnosed liver disease from drinking home-brewed liquor which she buys in Topsia. Manwara will not stop drinking, because the emotional pain is greater than the physical, and she no longer cares what happens to her. The decline of Manwara has been swift and shocking. She cries, the desolate tears of a woman who has become old in less than a year.

In the waste segregation unit where Manwara works, Naushad presents a striking contrast. He is about 30, and if he looks happy, he says, this is because his third child – a boy – has just been born. Naushad considers himself the most fortunate of men. He was a child waste-collecter – he used to roam all over Topsia with a jute sack, collecting bottles, papers, plastic and metal at random, and selling it for a pitiful few rupees to the retailers. Now he is employed at a fixed and regular wage, segregating waste which is collected in the godown and accumulates until it can be sold in bulk to the wholesaler. Naushad is delighted with the idea that waste, which destroyed his childhood, has become a source of hope to his own children.

Among the huts and industrial units on the road, a man covered in soot works with coal dust in a windowless brick building roofed with corrugated metal. The doorway is the only source of light and air. Inside, the black dust is stored in heavy polythene bags. There is a powdery deposit on the walls and the floor is covered with black sootfall, showing clearly the prints of the bare feet of the lone worker. The coal dust is used in rubber factories and for the retreading of tyres for vehicles, but it is also mixed with water and made into fuel cakes for domestic cooking. Mohammad Siraj is 40, but he looks much older, although the dark interior and the soot that obscures all but his eyes and teeth has no rejuvenating effect on his appearance. He wears a shirt and shorts and a baseball cap turned backwards. The coal dust comes from the coal depot in Howrah. It is put into bags there, and sold from this shed at 20 rupees per kilo ($0.50). Mohammad Siraj and his wife have five children. He works an eight-hour day, but has no protective mask against the dust. It is pitiable and surreal, this labour with dust, a primitive, Dickensian urban occupation. The air is full of particles that scintillate in the sunlight that pours in the door, a silvery particulate snowfall that lodges in every part of his body, and which he absorbs into mouth and lungs with every breath.

## XIV
## CAPTIVES OF WASTE

Close to this unit, a spacious bamboo enclosure is reached by a shallow downward flight of concrete stairs. It opens out into an extensive, privately owned yard in which plastic is sorted. Most workers are women. A heap of multicoloured waste, several metres high, is piled up against the back wall of the yard. Six women sit before big woven baskets of bamboo, each one specialising in the collection of various forms of plastic; an endless penitential labour in the face of a constantly replenished supply. It is a bleak sight, each woman crouching before her basket as though sitting at a gigantic banquet where the fare is inedible; a mockery of their daily experience of hunger.

At first, it is difficult to distinguish the objects heaped in promiscuous confusion; but as things are separated, they appear clearly as shampoo bottles, combs, toothbrushes, medical syringes, bottles of detergent, disinfectant, cleaning fluid, bowls, the shell of cellphones, soft drinks bottles, bags, domestic containers and vessels – so much discarded plastic that represents for the workers money that will put food into their mouths. Polymers that will be made into granules, coarse plastic chopped into pieces ready for melting and re-shaping. Plastic for balti containers, thin plastic for bags and plastic sheeting – the women recognise 15 different kinds of plastic, each one of which will be reincarnated in another form of itself. Only plastic, said one woman, laughing, is immortal.

Women earn between 80 and 100 rupees a day, men 100–150 rupees, although new workers receive less until they are able to distinguish the different varieties of plastic and can sort it appropriately. They work twelve hours a day, every day. Many are from Orissa. Some of the plastic waste comes from Bhubaneshwar in trucks, although most is collected from other parts of West Bengal. The owner is Oriya, which is why he brought many people from his home area.

They do not regard this site as one of captivity although they eat and sleep here, and, since their arrival, many have never been further than the market on the dusty roadside outside the compound. In a corner on the right-hand side are the women's 'quarters', while the men sleep on the left. Home is a primitive structure, a bamboo frame, with a ladder leading to an upper platform, a floor of wooden planks covered in plastic. Each woman has a quilt, which is neatly folded and stacked away in a corner. The roof is of corrugated metal on which rain and rats dance at night. Everything suggests impermanence and improvisation, yet some people have been here for many years. On a plastic sheet covering the compacted earth of the lower storey, two women are sorting light bulbs, separating the glass from the aluminium. Hazra Bibi came from Orissa 13 years ago. Her husband was a government employee, earning 10,000 rupees a month, but he divorced her. She is with her son, who came as a small child. He is now an adult. He has a black beard and is very pious. Hazra Bibi is proud that he says namaz five times a day. She had to leave the village because as a woman alone she had no means of livelihood. Her son grew up among these mountains of plastic, these streams of rubbish, this forest of used-up objects; a relentless labour of sorting and separating, work of inhuman futility. His religion is his refuge from chaos.

Tajara Bibi is from a village about 50 kilometres from Kolkata. She was also abandoned by her husband, but she came because her village was flooded and her parents' house submerged. After that, there was no work in the waterlogged fields. She earns about 400 rupees a week, and sends money home, not only for her parents, but also for her brother who was a rickshaw driver, but has fallen sick and cannot work. He is married with two children. Six people depend upon Tajara's slender income, most of which she remits to the village. She has been here for six years and manages to go home for a couple of days every two months. There are other women from her village who introduced her to the work. They also send home most of their earnings. Word of mouth and personal contact often determine people's labour, and sometimes semi-rural enclaves are formed in the city by people from the same village.

Outside the godown, Sanjuda Bibi, also from West Bengal, is sifting through a recently arrived truckload of plastic. As she turns it over with her feet, her eyes are on the lookout for anything of special value that might have found its way into the garbage. Her daughter, a little girl of about two, is eating from a thali, rice and dal. She sits on a rubbish sack. She receives food from the government Integrated Child

Development Scheme, but what kind of a life is it, asks her mother, to be brought up in a wasteland, a land of waste?

## XV
## AN EMERGING MUSLIM MIDDLE CLASS?

This is the most dramatic, but certainly not the whole, story of Topsia, which covers a wide area. On the edge of Topsia, there is a splendid new school set up by philanthropist Shaikh Shamsher Alam in 2002, specifically for the education of the children of the 'socially and economically deprived strata of the society.' Shaikh Shamsher Alam was from a lower middle class family in a West Bengal village. Encouraged to follow his education, he went to university and worked in the Government of India Income Tax Department where he is now an Assistant Commissioner. He invested everything he could in the Stock Exchange and made a considerable fortune, all of which has gone into the school. He says,

Children who go to government schools find the environment unattractive and punitive, a repellent to education. It was my intention to make an environment that drew children towards education, so that they would prefer school to home. I wanted to create an addiction to school. Many motivated parents think all they have to do is send their children to a private school, and then their responsibility is discharged. Perhaps a majority of private schools do not live up to their claims; the owners are often rapacious and unenlightened and their schools are often not officially recognised.

We are trying to provide a liberal education without compromising Islam. This involves showing parents that education is not just instrumental, that the making of a good human being and a responsible citizen is also the purpose of education. We have to overcome social traditions that claim religious sanction, but in fact have none. Local imams define and reinforce harmful customs. Their worldly knowledge is often scanty, their social understanding small.

We have 1260 students. In order to encourage the education of girls, the morning session is exclusively for them, while boys study in the afternoon. This is our contribution to Ward 66, one of the most deprived in Kolkata. Our fees are kept very low, and are waived for the very poor.

We met the teachers on the last day of the term before the summer vacation. There were about 30 or 40, mainly young women, animated by a sense of mission and possessed of an unusually purposeful energy. They are under no illusion about the task they face – not least, the resistance of parents to promises of education and its future benefits, by comparison with the immediate prospects of earnings from their children.

The school is situated in Rai Charan Ghosh Lane in Kolkata, a green meandering road, with the vestiges of original vegetation, bananas with their elliptical red flower, and the fresh tender growth of mango and guava trees. Here and there stand the mouldering houses of the old *bhadralok* of Kolkata, the superior and cultivated classes of Bengal; associated with a rather austere but high-minded way of life, overtaken now by the more showy wealth of globalism. Their conviction that they are the custodians of an imperishable Bengali culture has become strained in a world agog for novelty, sensation and the playthings of consumerism. One house in particular, painted green, with verandah and stone steps, peeling and semi-derelict, stands as a reminder of another city; submerged now, not only by hovels and hutments but also, in the last decade, by soaring concrete towers. Many of these are five or six stories high, constructed so close together that little light enters the windows, although uncollected garbage and refuse in the narrow passage-ways provide food for goats, chickens and wild leprous dogs. The buildings themselves flout (unenforced) planning regulations and are mostly illegal, but the rooms and apartments in them sell at steeply rising prices.

We were told by one of the residents of these flats:

People who live in the original buildings are paid to leave and pressure is brought by muscle-men to make sure they accept what is on offer. If you are very persistent, the promoters may offer you a flat on the third floor because this is cheaper. The value of the ground floor property is very high – 1200–1500 rupees per square foot, so that a 300 square-foot space would cost 3.5 lakh (more than $7,000); the first floor costs 1000–1200 rupees per square foot, the second floor 800–900 a square foot. It gets cheaper the higher you go. This is the opposite of the higher-class apartments, which become more expensive as they rise.

The educational dilemma became clear when we spoke to some of the people in Topsia, those inching their way painfully out of poverty; not quite middle class, because their position remains precarious, their livelihood threatened, their security not assured; but poverty for them is no longer quite the engulfing tragedy it has been.

In a chappals assembly unit I met Imran, a young man of 19, who left school at eleven and has worked here ever since. He was attaching the thongs, the strap and divider that go between the big and second toes (after it has been shorn of superfluous rubber by the women and girls of the canalside) to the sole of the slipper. Three holes have been bored in the sole, and Imran's job is to glue the flattened end of the three-cornered thong and push it through the three holes in the sole so that it sticks fast. He was working with a metal skewer that forced the thong, with its flattened end, through the opening, and then pushed it with his thumbs to secure it. He worked at such speed it was almost impossible to detect the movements of his hands, which hovered like dark butterflies over the material. Imran's father and two brothers are doing the same work.

The pairs of chappals rise into a heap two metres high. A second boy is working with Imran. The boys left school early because they are of greater value to their family as earners than as students: 'the labour value of children', as the economists call it. They work at great speed, and 100 dozen pairs pass through their dexterous hands each day. They make 1000 rupees a week. Imran says it is his purpose and duty to help his mother and father. By their combined labour, four years ago the family managed to buy two rooms in one of the new units. At that time, the property was cheap and the price was only 75,000 rupees ($1,500). Today it would be much more.

I calculated that if Imran left school at eleven and worked for four years, which was when the family bought their house, his contribution to the family income over that time would have amounted to 96,000 rupees (about $2,000) – more than enough to buy the small apartment outright. In that period, he would have worked on more than 2.5 million pairs of chappals. If these are sold in the retail shops at 25 rupees a pair, this amounts to 625 million rupees. Even when all workers employed in the strangely elaborate division of labour involved in the production of these simple articles have been paid, the owner's profit is considerable.

A tradition of child labour, therefore, makes more sense to the family than a prolonged period of study; and, indeed, the collective work of the family becomes the vehicle for their upward mobility. It is easy to see the reason for resistance to education, even among people who want to rise in the world: all the pieties about learning freeze on the lips, the more so since not only have Muslim crafts been systematically undermined but Muslims are also denied entry into much of the modern sector. The fragile security of their improvement is constructed on the shared effort of the family and its pooled income. A room in a building appears a safer bet than a hut, or even than a brick single-storey *kholabari*, in an informal settlement, for the obvious reason that if all illegal structures in Kolkata were to be demolished, it would leave a wasteland.

There are scores of these new buildings and, dark and uninviting though they appear, they offer the means to the creation of a new class of better-off Muslims, not quite middle class, but no longer exposed to the humiliations of poverty in the bustees.

## XVI
## EDUCATION OF GIRLS

In Topsia Road, we came to the Library and Free Reading Room. This is a government-subsidised amenity. The single room, with its metal cupboards and rows of books in Urdu, Bengali and English, had a long wooden table and a verse from the Qur'an, which, somewhat incongruously, said 'For every trial there is some form of testing, and for one trial, it is wealth. God has given wealth to test our sense of justice.' Such texts are displayed with no conscious sense of irony.

The librarian was stamping the day's papers with the blue oval of the library seal, which he first pressed onto an inkpad and then carefully brought down on the front page of each journal. To the question of who comes into the library, he

said, 'Students and local learned people.' He said he had
noticed one change in recent years: girls are beginning to
take education more seriously than boys. This is because
girls realise that if they study, they may acquire a skill that
gives them options for the future. Then, fearing that he had
said too much, he said 'I cannot speak because I am on
government duty.'

As if on cue, at that moment a group of schoolgirls came
into the library and filled the gloom with radiant life. What
had looked like a ritual facility set up in the minority area
for form's sake was immediately transformed into a place of
energetic enquiry, where young women come to study in safety
and silence. If the librarian was inhibited by his function,
the girls were under no such vow of silence. They offered a
swift diagnosis of the present state of things. 'Boys are more
fun-loving', was the general view, 'while girls are insecure.
Education will give us security in the future. Many boys get
good results, but they do not get opportunities for work.
There are thousands of unemployed graduates. The education
gap between boys and girls is closing. Boys are losing patience,
and are more ready to turn to crime or find illegal ways of
getting money, since the promise of livelihood has not been
fulfilled. Girls have not been through such an experience.'

The girls attend a government-supported Urdu-medium
school. Gulabshah is wearing a *niqab* and a black *salwar
kamiz*. Urdu is her favourite subject. Her father is retired,
and she has four sisters – two married – and one brother.
Her brother could not complete his education because of
financial problems; she appreciates her own opportunity
to do so. She works as she studies, making soft toys and
doing *mehendi*. She has a dream, which she doubts will ever

come true. She would like to work as an air hostess, but is sufficiently realistic to know it is implausible.

Daraksha's father is a 'service-man', but she does not know exactly what he does. (It is not uncommon to find that children have only the haziest notion of their father's occupation). Her parents support her study, and she hopes to be a teacher. Afim's father and mother are dead and she is taken care of by her older brother, who is 20 and makes a living in a factory that produces leather bags and wallets. He earns 4000–5000 rupees each month and is happy to sacrifice himself for his sister; she is very close to him, and recognises his selfless affection for the family. Two smaller brothers are studying. They live in a single room that belonged to their grandmother, so they do not have to pay rent. Sabra Jamil's father is a hawker, selling semi-precious stones for jewellery. Sabra has one brother and they live in a three-room apartment that they own. Her father wants her to become a software engineer, but she is unsure. Nazneen's family also have their own house. Her father works in a factory making purses and leather bags. She has one brother and one sister, and her ambition is to become a teacher. Shagufta Parveen's father is also working in a leather factory. She has one small brother and she wants to help other girls become educated as well.

Gulabshah, the most articulate and forthright of the group, says girls want to overtake boys 'so that we are free and not dependent.' She says they have always been poor. They have water and electricity in their houses but little more. These girls are part of a class climbing out of the most abject poverty, which brings new forms of uncertainty because their position is still precarious and haunted by a fear of losing what small advantage they have gained. It became almost a refrain: people repeatedly expressed the idea that poverty is like a close relative, as it can come and stay uninvited in our house at any time.

You do not have to look far in the surrounding streets to understand what they mean. The ground floor of an adjacent building opens out into a cavernous manufacturing unit that makes rubber fan-belts for cars. The rubber passes through a machine which thins and flattens it, and it is then treated with chemicals to make it resist the stress of continuous stretching. The finished product emerges in great sheets of black material which are cut into strips to form the fanbelts. There is no ventilation in the factory: the windows give on to neighbouring walls and, in any case, they are covered with a grimy deposit of rubber particles that also adheres to the machinery, dimming the two solitary striplights that shed their bluish pallor onto the shadowy concrete workspace. The workers are resting since it is the middle of the day: they lie on sheets of rubber, sacking and bags that contain chemicals. The air is thick with dust, which the sunlight in the doorway cuts as though it were solid matter. The men earn 600 rupees a week for an eight-hour day. There is occasional overtime, but at this moment business is down. I asked if they were not worried about inhaling the rubber dust or being exposed to the chemicals. They said they would be more worried if they had no money to feed their families.

## XVII
## EDUCATION AND PROGRESS

A dark concrete doorway, encumbered with vegetable waste and household detritus, led to three flights of stairs that were so low you had to duck in order not to scrape your head on the underside of the staircase above, before opening into an immaculate apartment in the process of being decorated. It had been plastered and painted white. The floors were tiled, the doors were carved and highly varnished, and the modern light-fittings filled the space with a cool brilliance. It is difficult to imagine a greater contrast than that between the squalor outside and these finely wrought rooms.

I met Syeda Sabrina Sameed, a 23-year-old who last year graduated with honours in English. Poised and graceful, she speaks a sweet and fluent British-English. Syeda said how much she enjoyed literature. She loved *Macbeth*, and especially enjoyed *Pride and Prejudice*. It struck me as strange that Jane Austen should resonate in this place so remote from Regency England; and yet, the marrying of daughters is a major family undertaking here, attended by social and financial calculations no less subtle than those of England in the early nineteenth century.

Syeda had just applied for the teacher training course run by the Assemblies of God. She had been interviewed the previous day. She was unsure whether she had passed – not because of any lack of qualification, but as a result of an exchange with the college principal during the meeting. 'I support wearing the burka, and I asked her if it would be all right for me to dress according to my wish and my faith. She told me that they did not allow the wearing of the burka in class. I asked her, "Can I at least cover my head?" She said "Is it absolutely necessary?" I told her "Yes, if it is a mixed class." She replied "Well if you must."' Syeda thought this discussion augured ill for acceptance. She was planning to visit the college that afternoon to find out whether or not she had been accepted.

Syeda's father had been listening to our conversation. 'There should be no full mixing of male and female', he said gravely. 'So much of freedom should not be given.' Syeda said 'I am willing to compromise. If I can cover my head, that will be enough.'

Syed Nasim Ahmed, Syeda's father, is a courteous man who was in the Indian Air Force and then worked as a service engineer with big companies – Crompton and Telco – servicing Air Force vehicles. He has lived in Topsia for 40 years and owns this building, of which his apartment forms the top floor. The rest is rented out to tenants. He fully supports the education of girls. 'Without education', he says, 'we are not human beings.'

> The Prophet said, "seek education from cradle to grave." I know what it means to be poor. I saw hunger and want as a child in Topsia. We lived in one room, my father was working in a small factory. I was the first in our family to struggle for education. I was able to study, and then I saw an advertisement for recruits into the Air Force in Bangalore. I applied successfully, and that helped me to build on the foundations and to continue learning. I have two sons and three daughters, two of whom are married; it has been my highest desire to see them accomplish whatever they can.

Syed Nasim Ahmed is socially conservative but educationally progressive. A distinctive feature of poor communities is that, in general, the more educated people become, the greater their tendency to religious observance and orthodoxy. Their support for education certainly does not involve any repudiation of religion. Far from it. Why this should be so was a recurring question, which prompted some interesting answers. A common response was,

... the more you know, the more you become aware of the sufferings of Muslims. It is not that the poor do not know, but their energies are absorbed simply by living, trying to survive. The more educated you are, the more you can see the wider context, in which a majority of Muslims remain in poverty and ignorance.

## XVIII
## THE CANALSIDE

We walked through the morose concrete canyons of Topsia, past drainage works intended to connect the empty-eyed concrete structures to an inadequate water system, past the long grey wall of the Mahindra Tyre factory and out towards the canal, from where we could see Topsia island and its rows of bamboo and chetai huts. On this side of the canal, there has been a shabby attempt at 'beautification': a grassless garden with pink granite benches, already crumbling, and a few dusty trees beneath which children are playing cricket. Everywhere along the stony track that follows the canal, there are heaps of stones, rubble, *kachra* and bricks. On a bare patch of the strand, we came across a strange spectacle: a dolls' graveyard, a pile of dismembered plastic dolls, some with hair still attached, heads, limbs and torsos, like the remains of a miniature massacre. Next to this disconcerting image, two men squatted over a metal griddle, a metre-square mesh, on which they appeared to be cooking what look like flat fish. On closer inspection, they were melting the soles of high-heel shoes. They heat the sole until the rubber is soft and pliable and then, with a sharp spike, remove the metal strip that supports the arch of the high-heeled shoes. On one side lies a pile of metal rods, on the other the filleted lower part of the shoe. From beneath the grill, ash eddies away on the wind and the embers are kindled to a bright scarlet. The men sell the iron for 2 rupees a kilo and the rubber for 1 rupee a kilo, and during the course of the day they make 200 rupees between them. The dolls are destined to be cut up in a machine, melted down and later re-appear as new playthings. The dolls were all coloured a high pink. Mohammad Yasim Khan stays nearby. He came from Bihar 20 years ago and has been doing this work for five years. His wife sells reconstituted coal nearby: each little black mound laid out separately on a length of jute, like pieces on a chessboard. The scene has the melancholy appearance of a joyless picnic.

While we were talking to Mohammad Yasim Khan, a phone call came from Syeda. She said her friend had been to the college and discovered that Syeda has been accepted on the teacher-training course. Her religious scruples had not counted against her.

We took a cycle-rickshaw along the rough road beside the canal. Dust and garbage were blowing in the wind, entering the small industrial units, lowering visibility and coating surfaces with drifting sand. On the left was the meandering greenish canal, but on the right the area opened out to a *jheel* or pond, on the other side of which loomed a power station, a squat grey building reflected in the turbid water. Next to the road, which rises as a causeway, there are grey shallows that used to be vegetable gardens but have now been abandoned, leaving an expanse of polluted mud.

Lalu, the rickshaw driver, has been pedalling for 28 years. He is in his 50s, but looked older. He is the owner of the cycle rickshaw and has to work a twelve hour day to make 120–150 rupees. He has two girls and three boys, and pays a rent of 330 rupees per month for his hut in Topsia. His boys are working in leather and plastic units. Lalu's life has improved over time, but that is mainly because his boys are now working and contributing to the family income. As a child, before he became a rickshaw driver, he had worked as an agricultural labourer on the jheel, but he was paid very little. He left the jheel to work in a plastic factory. There, he lost part of one hand in a machine: only a thumb and one finger remains. He was 18 then, and after that he had no choice but to turn to this – a labour of last resort.

We got down from the cycle rickshaw, and clambered up the reddish earthen slope to the East Metropolitan Bypass, where the speeding traffic occupied a different world to the scenes of tribulation from which we had just emerged. These are almost invisible from the raised road, which is not called 'fly-over' for nothing. We looked back over the houses on stilts which leak into the glassy canal. Through the misty afternoon, the concrete high-rises were marching towards the land on which the poor live. On every side they glower, waiting to pounce on the exiguous spaces that still remain to those who have nothing.

### The tragic irony of names

Islamic tradition calls upon the faithful to give beautiful and significant names to their children. The people of the Kolkata *bastis* have done so, although they cannot be unaware of the tragic discrepancy between name and aspiration.

| | |
|---|---|
| Aftab Alam | sun of the universe |
| Alamgir | one who controls the universe |
| Anwara | most brilliant, most beautiful |
| Ashraf | the best, noble |
| Asma | the name of the daughter of Abu Bakr, the first Muslim caliph after the death of the prophet Mohammad |
| Badal | cloud |
| Bahar | Spring |
| Daraksha(n) | illuminated |
| Deedar | to see, especially sacred objects |

| | |
|---|---|
| Dilshad | happy or fulfilled heart |
| Faiz | blessing |
| Gulabshah | king of roses |
| Haider Ali | *Father of Tipu Sultan, Raja of Mysore, who died fighting the East India Company* |
| Halima | gentle |
| Hamida | worthy of praise |
| Husna | beautiful |
| Irfan | wisdom, knowledge, enlightenment |
| Irshad | guide to the right path |
| Ismat | chastity |
| Jabeen | brow, forehead |
| Jan-e-Alam | soul or life of the universe |
| Jehanara | beauty of the world |
| Kaishan | (variant of Kahkashan) galaxy |
| Kamal | wonder or great achievement |
| Manwara | full of light |
| Masuda | prosperous, happy |
| Mehrun Nisa | pearl of women |
| Meraj | pinnacle (*also refers to the Prophet's ascent to heaven from Al-Aqsa mosque in Jerusalem*) |
| Moina | helper, aide |
| Mumtaz | well-known and respected |
| Munna | small |
| Nasim (f. Nasima) | morning breeze |
| Nazneen | beloved |
| Nurjehan | light of the world |
| Rahmat | mercy |
| Rashida | kind, affectionate |
| Rizwana | delighted, contented |
| Ruksana | shining, glittering |
| Sabra | patient, enduring |
| Sahari | dawn |
| Saida | lord, chief |
| Salim (f. Salima) | healthy, protected against calamity |
| Salma | submissive. (*In arabic, Muslim philosopher and interpreter of the Qur'an from Granada, who uses the name in poetry dedicated to his beloved*) |
| Sanjeeda | serious |
| Shahnawaz | the one gifted by a king |
| Shahzade | prince |
| Shakila | beautiful, well-formed |

| | |
|---|---|
| Shakir | grateful, contented |
| Shama | candle |
| Shamim | lofty, fragrant |
| Siraj | candle |
| Sitara | star |
| Sono | golden |
| Sultana | queen, ruler |
| Tarannum | melody |
| Taslim | accepted |
| Yasmin | jasmine |
| Zeba Anjum | beauty of stars |
| Zeeshan | doubly esteemed |
| Zeenat | beauty, elegance, adornment. |

*1* Mother and child, Topsia

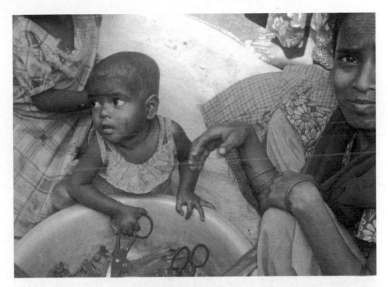

2    A future foretold

3    The library in Topsia

4   Unmaking shoes

5   The dolls' graveyard

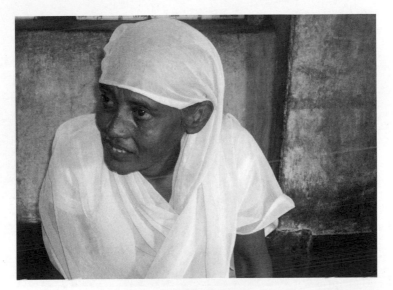

6   Rashida Begum

7   The right to education

*8* Topsia

*9* An apprenticeship

*10*  Street scene

*11*  A sandal-making unit

*12*   A childhood

*13*   The canalside at Topsia

# 2
# Injustice

## THE TEMPTATIONS OF INJUSTICE

Given the opportunities for wrongdoing, for making money and prospering through dishonest means, it is an astonishing tribute to young people that the great majority resist the temptation to do so. Mohammad Akbar is 25 years old. He lives in Topsia and goes daily to his place of work, a garment shop in Burrabazar. Even this job he does under a false (Hindu) name. 'People have told me to my face they will not employ Muslims,' he says. He had been unemployed for a year following an accident and, desperate to work, he changed his identity to secure a position for which he is paid 3000 rupees ($66) per month.

Mohammad Akbar studied until Higher Secondary, but left after Class X to support his family. He is a competent, intelligent young man who is frustrated by the lack of scope for improvement. There is no vocational training. He is the only boy in a family of four, and it is his responsibility to marry off his three sisters. He has no idea how he will manage it. There is, of course, a way, and when we met him he was deliberating whether or not to take it. During his time in Burrabazar, he has frequently heard of employment as a 'carrier' of smuggled goods to the city markets. 'It is a very tempting offer', he says. 'If I do it, I can increase my monthly earnings fivefold – to at least 15,000 rupees [more than $300].'

A significant number of educated Muslim young men have overcome their scruples. They travel to Hong Kong, Singapore and China, and bring back goods – mainly electronic items – which they supply to city markets. Mohammad Akbar is reluctant to join them because his life and upbringing have taught him to avoid illegal activities, but when these become the only outlet available to ingenuity and the desire to make a decent livelihood it requires a great deal of courage to refuse. He had not made up his mind and was still hopeful that he might find work compatible with his ability and understanding by fair means. Once you commit yourself to a life of illegality, there is no turning back. The future remains insecure, but then it is insecure already. It means changing one kind of uncertainty – to suffer quietly – for another; to risk exposure to the law and being branded criminal. Many young men spoke to us of this dilemma.

## II
## FALSE CASES

All Muslims know that youths are picked up at random, and paraded by the police as suspects in notorious cases, and indeed, they are sometimes killed in 'encounters', at best, frequently tried and imprisoned by means of perjury and fabricated evidence. While I was in Kolkata in June 2009, the *Telegraph* newspaper reported:

Ajijur Rahaman Sardar, son of Jamaluddin of Birmnagar, Majherpara Police Station, Basirhat, District North 24–Parganas, was shown arrested on June 22, 2007. For: Attempted armed *dacoity* [banditry] in Tiljala, Calcutta. Acquitted by court for want of evidence in 2008.

Ajijur Rahaman Sardar, son of Jamaluddin or Biramnagar, Majherpara Police Station Basirhat, District North 24–Parganas, was shown arrested on June 29, 2007, for alleged smuggling of RDX (explosive) into Lucknow on June 22–23, 2007. Status: lodged in Lucknow jail awaiting trial.

While in the custody of police in Tiljala, Sardar was alleged to have smuggled explosives into Lucknow. Such discrepancies are rarely reported in the press, although they come as no surprise to those for whom arbitrary arrest, imprisonment and punishment are part of the risk of being Muslim in India.

## III
### AFTAB ALAM ANSARI

The sequel to these laconic reports is rarely published. Some cases, however, become briefly notorious; although even the most flagrant injustices, the most obvious examples of 'mistaken identity', are briefly publicised and then absorbed into an institutionalised amnesia. Victims like Aftab Alam Ansari, wrongfully and ruinously accused of terrorist outrages in which he had no part at all, are expected to resume their life with minimal compensation and no recognition of the ordeal they have been through.

We met Aftab in the Oxford Book Store on Park Street in Kolkata. This was a neutral place, where we would be able to talk freely without distraction and without fear. We met him on a busy afternoon, in this part of Kolkata that he had never been to before. He was nervous and uneasy. He was accompanied by his mother, Ayesha Begum – and with good reason, since without her he would almost certainly not have been free to keep the appointment. She is the real hero of his story.

Aftab is a thickset young man, whose air of anxiety and dejection is certainly a consequence of his experience. The family came originally from Gulabazar, near Gorakhpur in Uttar Pradesh. Aftab's father was an employee of the Calcutta Electric Supply Company. When he died in 2002, Aftab 'inherited' his job. Aftab's family – two brothers and four sisters – were happy that he had secure employment, all the more so because he was the eldest and now the only earning member. Two sisters are married and two are studying, and they all live in a small *kholabari* house (a single-storey house with a tiled roof).

Ayesha Begum was at home when Criminal Investigation Department officers, posing as bank officials of the Unit Trust of India Mutual Funds, came looking for Aftab, who was at work. They told her that her son had offered to act as loan guarantor and they wanted to interview him. The date was 26 December 2007. Since he was not at home, they asked for a photograph, which his mother gave them. They also had a secret camera with which they took pictures of the house. They showed her a photograph and asked her to identify the individual as her son. It was a picture of someone unknown to her, so she told them she did not recognise him.

When Aftab reached home, he was met by a crowd of men standing in a circle around the house. They arrested him without asking any questions, and hustled him into a car, which sped off to a destination somewhere near the airport. They thrust him inside a flat on the second floor of an apartment building.

One officer said to me 'Your name is Mukhtar, alias Raju.' I said, 'That is not my name. My name is Ansari.' They beat me. 'No, no, you are a terrorist. You belong to HUJI, Harkat-ul-Jihad al-Islami. You are an active member and were the mastermind of the serial blasts in Uttar Pradesh in 2006, including at Varanasi, where 28 people were killed.

Aftab was implicated in all the blasts. They said to him, 'You were in Bangladesh.' He has no passport and has never been outside India. Aftab, shocked and frightened, was utterly at the mercy of their certainty that he was someone else:

They showed me some photographs and demanded that I identify them. 'Who is he? Who is he?' I said I didn't know. They insisted these were my associates. I was told they had identified me as Mukhtar, alias Raju. The officer took off his belt and beat me with it repeatedly.'

Despite Aftab's repeated denials and his terror at what was happening, senior Indian Police Service officers, including the Deputy Inspector General and other high-ranking police officers, called a press conference. They gave the official version – that the ringleader of the Uttar Pradesh blasts had been apprehended and was in custody. The Chief Minister later expressed his happiness that the police had done such fine work and made such a big catch.

Imran Ahmed Siddiqui was present at the press conference. He said everyone was congratulating the police, and they were receiving text messages from other police forces all over India praising them for their cleverness and courage. The press reported with enthusiasm the 'prize catch' of a 'key Harkat-ul-Jihad al-Islami operative in a joint operation by West Bengal CID and the Uttar Pradesh Special Task Force. Further investigation revealed that he supplied RDX (explosive) for carrying out explosions at the Shankat Mohan Temple in Varanasi.'[7] 'He [Aftab] reportedly told the sleuths during interrogation at the CID headquarters in Bhabani Bhavan that he had gone to Pakistan a few years ago to attend a training camp organised by militant outfits.'[8]

I spent two days in the flat and was then taken to the CID head quarters in Bhabani Bhavan, where I was beaten again and then asked to become a government witness. If I did, I would be spared. The Special Task Force were looking for a guy called Mukhtar, who was supposed to have come from Bangladesh on a visa to Kolkata. The arrest warrant was in the name of this Mukhtar, and they wanted me to confess that this was my identity. The Special Task Force people took me by road to Varanasi. They tied my hands with a rope and kept me in the back of a Tavera. We stayed two hours, and then I was driven to Lucknow. There I was subjected to third degree torture, electric shocks, I was stripped naked and they beat me with a rubber *lathi* and a bat. They poured water over me and beat the soles of my feet. They said if I confessed the torture would cease. I kept asking them to check with my office, my employer and neighbours to investigate my circumstances, but they took no notice.

I said I didn't know anything. I didn't even know what RDX [Research Department Explosive] was. How could I accept what they are saying? I did nothing. I had to bear it. In the Lucknow detention centre, the officers asked me why I had gone to Gorakhpur in March and then in May of the preceding year. I said I had gone to get married in Gorakhpur. One officer asked me if 'getting married' was a code for organising serial blasts. The Special Task Force officers brought the suspects who had originally identified me, people already in custody. They admitted they had never seen me before. This did not shake their conviction that I was who they thought I was, *who they wanted me to be*. I was in a state of terror – and I was supposed to be the terrorist. I was taken to a court and accused of serial blasts in Varanasi, smuggling

RDX into Uttar Pradesh and setting off the three blasts in Gorakhpur in May 2007. In jail I was given bread made of coarse wheat flour, rice full of stones and tasteless vegetables. No one was allowed to meet me and I was given no exercise. I was sick and I wept. I could not believe what was happening. My ordeal lasted 17 days.

Ayesha Begum takes up the tale. She has the same sad look as her son, but she weeps more freely, removes her glasses to wipe her eyes with the edge of her beige-coloured saree.

The police raided our small room. It is just 210 square feet. They ransacked it. They searched all the electric appliances in the house, took them apart. They broke down the door of the almirah. I was crying and saying, 'We are not like that. We are ordinary working people.' They scolded and abused me.

On the day that her son was taken to Lucknow, Ayesha followed him by train. She knew no one in Lucknow. For two days, she stayed in a small guest house, but then her money ran out, so she lived on the pavement for seven days. 'I slept under a tree. It was winter and very cold. There was a roadside eatery nearby. I took some burning coal from their *chulha* to warm myself.' She found no lawyer willing to take the case. Even lawyers fear association with 'terrorists', particularly when the case has already been pre-judged and certified by the international media.

I came back to Kolkata. I collected all Aftab's papers, his school certificates and medical certificates, and also a programme from his office, where he had signed the register as being present on the day they said he was in Bangladesh. In fact, on that very day, when they said he travelled from Bangladesh, he had reported sick, and gone to the office doctor. He was with the doctor at the moment when the blasts actually took place. He had a certificate to prove it. The name was his real one, not the one they had arrested him under. As soon as the story was announced on TV, and I saw that Aftab had been arrested under the name of Muktar, I took all his papers to a relative's house for safekeeping. If the authorities had taken possession of them, they might have been destroyed in order to sustain the claim that Aftab was indeed this Mukhtar.

I approached a lawyer in Kolkata, and showed him all the papers. He agreed to take the case. I told him, the day of the blast, my son was sick. On the day he was supposed to appear before the court in Lucknow, they did not produce him because, they said, if they did so there was a danger he would flee. His associates would make an attempt to release him and create a security problem. He was kept out of sight. I wanted to see him because they were not producing him. It was a nightmare, imagining what they had done to him.

The police gave her the address of the jail where he was being held. She went and asked if she could see her son. She was told to wait. 'Your son is not here.' 'Why? Where is he?' 'Your son is not here. Leave.' Ayesha returned to the lawyer, who took her to the judge. A date was finally fixed for a meeting. It would take five days.

I stayed on the pavement. I had no money. I had to return to Kolkata without seeing him. I took loans from friends and neighbours. His sister's marriage was scheduled at this time, but because of all the publicity, the marriage was cancelled. Who would want to marry into the family of a terrorist? The TV channels and the newspapers came asking for information. We had become known nationally, and for the worst possible reasons. While I was in Kolkata, trying to raise more money, someone from a newspaper visited me, and told me my son had been acquitted. I was crying. I scolded the journalist and said to leave me alone.

Ayesha Begum called the lawyer and was given confirmation that Aftab had been acquitted. It was the responsibility of the police to bring him to Kolkata, but Ayesha was suspicious. She did not trust the police to bring him home safely, so she said that she would go to Lucknow and have him released into her custody. 'I went that night on the train to UP. He was still in jail. They brought him out to me. I had never in my life been in a jail, and neither had he.'

When Aftab was arrested, he was suspended from the company, a government undertaking. After his release, he was re-instated,

> But I am always scared. My mother will not let me go anywhere alone. At the time of my arrest, I had been married only a few months. When my wife heard what had happened, she fell unconscious and hit her head against some iron.

Aftab is the eldest child, and the family is his responsibility. His mother was his only help when he was in need. It was her foresight and her persistence that saved him. Without her, he can only imagine what might have happened. He re-lives the ordeal every day. All other relatives broke their ties with him; even though they had known him all their life and could not even suspect him of being guilty, fear drove them away. False accusations isolate individuals; they are quarantined by fear from family and neighbourhood, and this makes it more difficult to examine critically the case that authority has made against them.

After the story of Aftab's ordeal had been widely circulated and he had been completely exonerated, the Chief Minister called him to the Writers' Building in Kolkata (the seat of government). He asked Ayesha Begum how much she had spent in helping her son. Ayesha told him it was upward of 1 lakh. ($2000). She had sold everything to rescue him. The Chief Minister's response was 'Did you keep the receipts?'

It was absurd. My son was being tortured and accused of monstrous crimes. How would I go round asking for receipts? I had other things on my mind. I just wanted to do everything to get back my son. In the end, they gave us 30,000 rupees (About $650). That was called 'compensation'. How do you compensate ruined lives? They had taken Aftab's ring and wristwatch. He got them back only after he had seen the Chief Minister.

The Chief Minister was also Home Minister. It was his policemen who had tortured Aftab; perhaps so small a recompense was offered because Aftab had revealed the incompetence and cruelty of the system. No human rights organisation took up his case. Aftab's grandmother used to stay with the family. Six months ago, she died. They had spent 75,000 ($1500) on treatment for her. Aftab earns Rs7,500 (US$180) a month. He is now 27.

The press reported with relish the 'Cop goof-up on Calcuttan'. The police told the *Telegraph* his arrest was 'a case of mistaken identity.' The violence he had suffered was sanitised by bland police statements: 'During the course of investigations, it transpired that he was not the person we were looking for.'

How could they have made such an error? Many bloggers questioned whether it was an error. There was no other male member of the family. They lived in wretched conditions. Was he targeted because he was alone and unprotected? Was he informed against by a malicious neighbour? There is always pressure on the police to find someone – anyone – in the wake of any terrorist outrage. The fightback came from an unexpected quarter, a mother who found great inner strength, a barely literate woman who would not meekly accept what the highest representatives of the Indian state chose – and on the flimsiest evidence – to believe. But why would they single out Aftab? If the police had wanted to show the world how they had triumphed over a dangerous terrorist, why did they not arrest a known criminal and shoot him in a false encounter, as happens in more 'civilised' parts of India?

Arundhati Roy, writing of Gujarat and the mob violence unleashed against Muslims with the encouragement and support of the state government following the death of 58 Hindus burned in a railway coach carrying pilgrims from Ayodhya, says,

> Under this relentless pressure, what will most likely happen is that the majority of the Muslim community will resign itself to living in ghettos as second-class citizens, in constant fear, with no civil rights and no recourse to justice. What will daily life be like for them? Any little thing, an altercation in a cinema queue or a fracas at a traffic light, could turn lethal. So they will learn to keep very quiet, to accept their lot, to creep around the edges of the society in which they live.

This is not prophecy: if it is already a fairly accurate account of the lives of many poor Muslims in West Bengal, where there is a CPI(M) government, it is not difficult to imagine how it must be in places where they are not defended by the brave 'secularists' in power.

After he has told his story, Aftab and his mother are both subdued and tearful. A group of three men walk past us, and he visibly flinches, half expecting to be challenged to give an account of himself. We go to the bookshop cafe for tea and cakes. Aftab continues to talk, although his conversation is now more reflective. Aftab was brought up by his grandfather, who also used to work in the Calcutta Electricity Supply Company. His father then took over, and then Aftab followed the family tradition. He stayed at school until he was 18. He is now following a degree course, through the Indira Gandhi distance learning university; grimly enough, in humanitarian studies. Since his incarceration and torture, he is unable to climb because his feet were damaged by the beatings to the soles.

Aftab had originally planned to join the army. His instinct, he says, was to defend his country, but he was prevented from doing so because at that time his father died. His preferred career would have been to fight for the country which had declared him 'anti-national.' The authorities had said they had evidence that he had been not only to Bangladesh but also to Pakistan, and that he had taken training in Afghanistan. 'Mastermind', he says sadly. 'The only thing I have to mastermind now is how to put my life together again.'

It was an immensely sad meeting, despite the inspiration of Ayesha Begum, her love and courage. No one was ever called to account for the operation against him. It is enough to be Muslim to be picked up at random, to be accused of atrocities or to be shot in the street in a faked 'encounter' – that oddly poetic word, which indicates a tryst or lovers' meeting, and which has come to be used as a euphemism for police actions against alleged terrorists.

Muslims, especially poor Muslims, have become victims of a malign conspiracy of unbelonging; the further effects of the 'Kashmirification' of all Muslims in India, and a phantom Pakistan to which they are believed to owe allegiance. As a consequence, anyone is liable to be called militant, ultra, infiltrator, fundamentalist, extremist, terrorist – a considerable and interchangeable lexicon that evolved in Kashmir to legitimise the brutalisation of young men in particular. In some parts of India, notably Modi's Gujarat, this process is far advanced; but it seems that West Bengal, sheltering behind a threadbare secular ideology, is not immune from the creeping stigmatisation of Muslims, all Muslims.

# 3
# Beniapukur

It was just before sunset when we first went to Beniapukur. The shadow of evening had reached the narrow thoroughfares while the sky was still silvered by the dying sun, and in small courtyards where women sat on the threshold, a little liquid light was trapped. Here, we met an attractive-looking young man with long hair escaping from beneath his Muslim *topi*.

The lower part of both his arms was missing. He told us he had a small shop, where he sold frills for girls' and women's dresses. He used to travel in the train from Kolkata to Mumbai to beg; and because people felt sorry for him, he managed to accumulate enough to start his own business. He originally worked in a plastics factory where, one day, he spilled adhesive onto his hands which caught fire and burned him so badly he had to undergo amputation. He was not telling the truth – and why should he? People who have known him all his life say that as a child he stole something. His mother, a very pious Muslim, wanted to teach him a lesson. She bound his hands and arms, and pretended to set fire to the bandages; but the match fell and the fire ran out of control until it had burned him beyond recovery. Intending simply to frighten him into virtue, she scarred him for life.

# I
# THE POLICE THANA

We walked unchallenged into Beniapukur police station. It was an austerely functional place – metal desks, concrete floors and creaking chairs. Stacks of files in curling brown covers stood on shelves, with dust several millimetres thick; the frayed and unconsulted records of forgotten, and probably trivial, crimes. In the lock-up, behind a grille that looked like the closed entrance to a lift, two boys accused of some small theft were sitting on wooden stools. They looked bored and hopeless, and from behind the bars arose a smell of urine and sweat, odours of poverty. In the stillness of the afternoon, the officers at their desks were inactive – overcome, it seemed, by lassitude. The ceiling fans gently stirred papers on spikes and files weighted down with stone paperweights, and a little dust danced in the slice of sunlight that forced its way through a smudged window. The place looked like a police post in some somnolent province, rather than at the heart of a metropolitan city of India. We had hoped to meet a Muslim police officer who would talk to us about crime in the city, but these districts of Kolkata do not look like the sites of significant criminality which many claim they are. Perhaps, Imran suggested, to see the real movers and shakers of the criminal world, we would have to go to the five-star hotels and upmarket Alipur.

Later, we had an opportunity to speak with a Muslim policeman, Mohammad Shakir (not his real name), in another part of the city. He is in his early 50s, married with five children, and has been in the Kolkata police for over 30 years. He knows that his colleagues speak disparagingly about him. They look down on him and do not trust him, but, since he has been working in this hostile atmosphere for so long, he is used to it. When they address Muslims, his colleagues call them '*katua*', which is a contemptuous word for circumcised men. Mohammad Shakir says he is always aware of their distaste, even though they do not always express it openly. 'I once heard them saying that I am not what I appear. They were saying I was a fundamentalist because I say namaz five times a day and do not drink.'

Mohammad Shakir speaks of 'communal undercurrents' even in the postings of policemen.

My colleagues are reluctant to go out with me to a place where there has been an incident. They question my efficiency because of my beliefs. I joined the force, because I wanted to serve society. I had the qualifications to become a teacher, but I chose the uniform because I wanted to help make sure people got justice. It did not occur to me that I would be seeking justice on my own behalf within the police.

I have no choice but to work with people who despise my religion. I try to talk to them about the tenets of Islam and how Islam is incompatible with terrorism. This is not new in Kolkata. At the time of the riots in Topsia and Tangra in 1992, one officer was accused by his colleagues of sending relief materials only to camps where Muslims had taken shelter. The allegations were unfounded, but no senior policeman defended him.

Mohammad Shakir has been posted to most Muslim areas of the city at one time or another. Of all of the fears of people in those areas, the greatest is of being picked up by the police.

Police visit areas like Topsia, Tiljala, Tangra and other Muslim areas only when they want to make an arrest in connection with some case or other. Muslim youth with no criminal record are picked up at random and detained illegally, sometimes tortured. I have observed it myself and I have protested often, but it is the norm. Nobody will listen to me and I'll be accused of being communal if I make any effort to support members of the Muslim communities.

The police know about the drug dens and the criminal activities, but they keep silent on them as a result of political orders. Government has successfully broken the economic livelihoods of Muslims. They have also not opened a single school in Tiljala, Topsia, Tangra.

The injustice extends even to prisons. In the city's two jails – Presidency Correctional Home and Alipore Correctional Home – the authorities have even stopped prisoners from receiving or sending letters in Urdu. The authorities assume that a letter in Urdu must have been sent by some terrorist group, and that the recipient is one of their henchmen.

In the light of such testimonies, it is clear that government reports on the under-representation of Muslims in the institutions of state are no unplanned omission, but are a consequence of policy which is nowhere stated but everywhere visible. Mohammad Shakir does not have many years left before retirement, but he fears for the fate of a new generation of Muslims in this, apparently most secular, city in India.


## II

## GOVERNMENT SERVICE

We came to a by-lane, passed through a narrow entry and emerged into a small stone courtyard. In one corner there were two brick cells with a space between them full of clutter, brooms, buckets and rags. The little rooms were enclosed by a metal grille and padlocked from the inside. From this it was clear that the owner was at home. Eventually Mohammad Abdur Rouf looked out, cautious and distrustful, to see who was calling. He unlocked the door and came out onto the pavement in front of the house. A neighbour produced two or three plastic chairs.

Mohammad Abdur Rouf is in his 60s. He walks with the help of a metal crutch, as a result of a broken femur. Distinctly frail, but speaking with great vehemence, he said 'It is a crime to be known as a Muslim in India. What is India after 60 years of Independence? There is no justice in court, no rule of law, no democracy.' He looked defiant, as though waiting for contradiction. Neighbours gathered on the threshold of the one-storey brick-built houses which face his cramped cabins – there are about half a dozen small houses in the compound. The people, watchful and impassive, said nothing. These are his tenants, but he feels threatened, beleaguered, locked in his own cell, just as he has been immured in the injustice that has haunted him for over a quarter of a century. 'People are even trying to get me out of my small quarters. They want my property. They have been throwing brickbats, and dumping rubbish outside my gate. Just look, you will see how they have treated me.'

This is not, however, the origin of his grievance.

25 years ago, I was selected for employment in the Food and Supplies Department. The date was 5 May, 1982. I received my letter of conditional appointment from the Government of West Bengal. All that was required was that I should get my police verification form and a medical certificate stating that I was fit for work. I replied according to the requirements and submitted all the relevant papers. Nothing happened. I waited and inquired, inquired and waited. For years I heard nothing. Finally I got my letter confirming me in my post. The date of that? 29 November 2007, more than a quarter of a century after my appointment. I presented myself at the place where I was to work. I was to be an Assistant Sampler in the Food and Supplies Department of West Bengal. That meant going round to public eating-places, dhabas and restaurants and taking samples that would be sent

to a laboratory for analysis. I am a Bachelor of Science from Bangabasi College at Sealdah. I had been called for interview immediately after I applied for the job. I supplied all the details they demanded. The police came to my home one month later to verify my identity. Then I had no communication for 25 years. A quarter of a century. When I eventually did get admission to my office, I worked for 41 days. By this time I was over 60 and due for retirement.

What happened? The police came, but they never submitted their report. Why? They wanted to implicate me in false cases. It has been a bitter experience. I stayed here with my mother. She died in the year I should have been appointed. Since then I have lived in silence and in solitude.

There is also a deeper reason for this neglect. Abdur Rouf's elder brother wanted the property. Abdur Rouf is the *theka* tenant (holder of government land), and he draws rent from the six houses that comprise the family inheritance. His brother, together with two Hindu tenants, tried to evict him in collusion with the police. It was also at the instigation of his brother that attempts were made to implicate him in false cases. His brother had promised the police a share in the yield from the property when it was sold.

Abdur Rouf says,

Everything is ruined. I have lost everything. I could not marry and have a family because my only income was the small rent from these houses. I have spent my whole life going from office to office, trying to find out why my appointment had not been confirmed; and every time they sent me from one place to another. It was only when I eventually met the Speaker of the West Bengal Assembly in 2007, the local MLA [Member of the Legislative Assembly] and also a Muslim, that anyone recognised the injustice I have suffered over so many years. He took up the matter. I sent him the papers and he called the Food and Supplies Department. It was only after he had intervened that

I received confirmation that I had indeed been appointed. I worked
for one month and eleven days. I earned 2867 rupees for the 11 days
and 7869 rupees for the month I worked. I earned 10,000 rupees out
of what should have been a lifetime of honest labour.

Abdur Rouf's case was taken to an industrial tribunal as
a result of the intervention of the Speaker. Despite the
obstructive tactics of the state administration, the tribunal
found in his favour and the court ordered that he should
receive a full pension by way of compensation for the work he
was never allowed to do. So far, he has received nothing. The
direction of the court was ignored by the state government.

Abdur Rouf had received his letter in May of 1982. The
police visited him in June. They could and should have
given him clearance then. The false case lodged against him
by his brother came in September of the same year. These
fabricated charges hung over him until 2001, when they were
all dismissed by the court as baseless. It took two decades to
show what should have been obvious from the beginning.
Abdur Rouf says that once cases are filed in the court, they
take on a life of their own. His story – like that of many
other people – had a distinct whiff of Dickens, reminiscent
of Jarndyce and Jarndyce, where people literally grew old, as
Abdur Rouf has grown old, waiting for a resolution delayed
beyond endurance. His brother died in 1997, but the cases
in which he had been complicit maintained an afterlife in the
twilit bureaucratic labyrinth in which they had taken refuge.
Abdur Rouf is contemptuous of the Minorities Commission,
to whom he had long ago taken his grievance. They have no
power to act and can give no relief, is his verdict.

This does not mark the end of his sorrows. He is alone and
vulnerable. There are six rooms standing on 5 kattas of land

(1 katta is 720 square feet). These yield a rent of only 500 rupees. Developers have their eye on the land. Some tenants are colluding with these people, who have encouraged them to withhold their rent. The developers have promised them improved accommodation in a high-rise block as a reward for getting Abdur Rouf out of his home.

> People are throwing garbage and stones. I hear them on my roof. I do not know what I have done to deserve such treatment. I used to go regularly to the *mazar* or shrine. I say namaz five times a day. I read the Holy Qur'an and the Hadith every day. It is a crime to be a Muslim in India. That is the only possible conclusion.

## III
## THE FRUSTRATED AND SELF-TAUGHT

These communities are full of people of repressed intelligence and wasted talent, compelled to do work they find repugnant and a life which denies them fulfilment. In Beniapukur we met Gulam Arif, an excitable, earnest, self-taught man in middle age, who would have been an intellectual if he had had the opportunity to study. Thin and voluble, he quickly told the story of his life. He lived among poor people as a child, and has spent a lifetime thinking of how poverty can be relieved. Gulam Arif is a mechanic, earning 3000 rupees ($75) a month. He lives in a single room with his younger brother, who works in a chappal factory and earns 600 rupees a week. 'I am a bachelor', he says. 'I was born here, and so was my father. My grandfather came from Bihar in 1912. I have no family and made no marriage. My mother was bedridden for 26 years and I looked after her till she died.' Stories, sometimes compressed into a few brief phrases, evoke suffering and selflessness, a cramped heroism confined in mean tenements. The slums are full of examples of an uncelebrated sense of duty and commitment.

Gulam Arif has a plan for poor relief. He says,

Baitul mal is an Islamic concept of welfare, of providing help to the needy. This should be established in every community, every ward in Kolkata. It is a form of self-help. You need the infrastructure to administer it. You can start with small sums of money – 2 rupees multiplied by 1000 creates a lot of money and, once it is set going, it continues to accumulate wealth. No individual holds it. It is paid regularly into a central bank. Then, when people in distress apply, all that is required is two witnesses to attest to their poverty and they will receive a payment according to their need. It is a pledge to all who may fall into want at any time – sickness, unemployment, especially for people whose family have died or are absent. For 23 years I have been advocating this. When I say it on the street, I am talking to the air, who will listen? But if I am dressed in robes and chant it as a mantra by the riverside, everyone will come and pay homage and say yes, yes, this is what the world needs.

# IV
# INTELLECTUAL DISCUSSION

In a neighbouring street, we visited Sayeed Uddin Ahmed. He has lived in Beniapukur all his life and has been a city councillor for the ruling Communist Party of India (Marxist). He is now elderly, and he reflects on the growing purposelessness of the Left, adrift in West Bengal, having adapted itself to what it likes to call the realities of global capitalism. His conversation is marked by a faint shadow of progressivism, the remnants of an ideology he has forfeited, but to which no adequate alternative has been formulated. He says,

The Muslim community is backward, but there is a slow awakening. Education is the pathway to social change. I have studied my community. I know it well.

The media teach the dogma of easy money. Every luxurious thing is supposed to be easy to avail, but it demands money. To earn money, they go to any limit ... In this corporate world, these malls lure them, so for a bit of money, instead of going to higher studies, they go to call centres, which have destroyed a younger generation. When a man is tired, and must bow down to the great of the world, he seeks solace in illusions. Illusion becomes the source of hope. He is then a captive of himself. People who are below the poverty line see all the things that the rich buy, and whether or not they have the resources, they will by hook or by crook get it to answer their desires.

Sayeed Uddin Ahmed says that poverty has always existed, exists still and always will exist. I observed that such fatalism was not quite what is expected from a member of the Communist Party. If we can no longer even imagine or dream of a world without poverty, we have become much poorer than we ever dreamed it possible to be. He smiled, a look of disorientation, a man living in a world of broken certainties and fragmenting morality. It is easy to see how, out of the ruins of secular ideology, the houseless spirit turns back to older stories of salvation. Sayeed Uddin Ahmed is a man trapped between the dead language of a Communism disconfirmed by long and bitter experience, and the vibrant appeal of an Islam which is proof against any such disavowal.

We had a number of similar conversations with CPI(M) party members, functionaries or intellectuals. There was a strong feeling of the exhaustion of a project that had transformed the lives of many rural poor people in the early years of Communist rule. But their support of the unions and the frequent strikes and demonstrations, and a sustained campaign against the capitalist class, effectively ruined the old industrial base of Kolkata. Amartya Sen observed, 'The industrial agitation [of the CPI(M)] may have given the workers more rights, but they lost many more rights by the industries withdrawing from Kolkata.'[9] The CPI(M), in a perverse epic of destruction and reconstruction, laid waste its industry and then sought to re-introduce it into West Bengal; in the process, taking land – some of it earlier given to sharecroppers and landless peasants – with only meagre compensation for their loss, and offering it to foreign and domestic industries (Nandigram and Singur became synonymous with callous expropriation). The CPI(M) has alienated many of its former supporters. At the same time, it made a bid to attract IT companies, and has successfully competed with other metropolitan cities with the construction of 'Science City'. Having abandoned its anti-capitalist rhetoric, its ideology became indistinguishable from that of the dominant developmental paradigm.

There has been overall economic improvement in Kolkata; but its Muslim minority has gained neither in skills nor in security, for the reasons we have seen – the handicraft and artisanal occupations they follow are liable to be wiped out by imports or mass-produced goods, and the buildings they inhabit exist on the margins of legality.

## V
## THE SEX TRADE

We gained some insight into the sex trade in the specifically Muslim bastis. Most of the sex industry is concentrated in Sonagachi and Kalighat, and there is no dearth of sex workers from these poor communities who find a livelihood there. But there is also a small thriving business around Park Circus. In the late afternoon, we sat in a spacious restaurant and hotel that stood open to the main road. We observed that there were very few customers, but many employees. At the entrance to the hotel, a strange sight presented itself. A strikingly attractive young girl, no more than 16 or 17 years old, appeared, looking as though she were uncertain about coming inside. She was dressed simply, but ceremonially, in what looked almost like bridalwear. She was accompanied by two young men, who left her standing just inside the restaurant and sat down at the table where Ali, Imran and I were drinking tea. They were immediately friendly. Perhaps with an eye to the prospect of a foreigner, they wanted to introduce us to the young woman. Without a word being spoken, their intention was clear. When it became plain that we were not going to respond, they did not leave. They were both gay. The younger man – perhaps in his early 20s – was taken with Imran and asked for his mobile number. He said to Imran, 'Are you married?' When Imran said that he was, the man answered, 'I like married men.' Imran subsequently received a number of calls asking for a date. Meanwhile the girl was left to the curious gaze of passers-by. She became quite distressed. The young men got up to leave, and took her by an outer staircase to the upper storey from which they had descended. The lack of customers in the restaurant became self-explanatory.

Later, Imran contacted the young man who had given him his telephone number. Posing as a potential client, he asked if he could introduce him to a girl. They arranged a meeting in a public park, a piece of parched grassy land close to Tiljala.

There, he was introduced by his acquaintance to Yasmeen, a young woman of 21 who lives in Beniapukur. She studied up to Class V in a Kolkata Municipal school, but had to discontinue her studies because her father, a tailor, could not afford to enroll her into a secondary school. In 2006, Yasmeen's father was critically injured in a road accident and his left leg had to be amputated. Yasmeen, as the eldest of four sisters, had to work as a maidservant to help support the family. She was paid 500 rupees a month ($11). Somehow, the family survived.

A chance meeting with a woman in south Kolkata, who owned two beauty parlours, changed her life. She was offered work in a parlour at 3000 rupees a month ($65), and readily agreed. She was shocked to learn that she had to cater to men in what was advertised as a beauty parlour for women. She had to give them a full body massage. She decided to quit the job, but on reflection, realised that she had few other options. Several other girls from poor families were doing the same work.

After two years, Yasmeen joined a beauty parlour in Tollygunge. She was befriended there by two customers who lured her into a different world. They told her if she became a part-time sex worker, she could earn 20,000 rupees a month. (almost $500). She overcame her reluctance and now earns between $300 and $500 a month. Her 'friends', who work as pimps, have contacts with several guest houses in the city. They arrange clients for her and receive commission. After the deal has been fixed, they accompany Yasmeen to the designated hotel or guest house. She spends two hours with the customer in the hotel room while her friends move around outside, then takes her fee and emerges from the hotel where the pimps collect her in a taxi. She pays them half of the 3000 rupees she has been paid.

> If my family members see me when I am working, they will not recognise me. I wear a salwar kamiz at home, but here I put on jeans and T-shirt when I meet clients. They won't pay 3000 rupees to a girl in a salwar kamiz.

One of her friends said, 'The dress code is important in this profession.' This is because the traditional Muslim dress is regarded as chaste and desexualised. Jeans and T-shirt are associated with Western imagery, they are exotic and uninhibited, and in the clothes she wears there is an implicit promise to the client. 'My family is very happy. And they do not ask too many questions. I do not need to work fixed hours. They [her pimps] contact me on my cellphone whenever my services are required.'

Her 'friend', Rahul, who lives in Lake Gardens and is now in his early 30s, originally failed his graduation examination. He took up work in guest houses as a receptionist and got to know girls who worked in beauty parlours; by recruiting them, he then started his own business. 'We go with the girls to guest houses. People take us to be friends and are not suspicious. This is the only business that requires no investment.' He has a list of cellphone numbers in his mobile.

> There are many Muslim girls who need money to sustain their families. There are now hundreds of beauty parlours and massage centres in the city. Some advertise in the press. Girls from Topsia, Tiljala, Tangra work in these places. They come from poor families. When they grow up, they tell their parents they are working as a help in hotels or in a garment factory. Family members often know that this is not true, but they do not choose to complain or investigate too closely.

## VI
## MUSLIM AND GAY

There are lesbians and gay men in all societies and cultures, although in some their ability to express themselves is highly circumscribed. I had met Kamal in Kolkata some time before we prepared this book, but he, too, was influenced by the Bihari exile culture of Kolkata's poor communities. Kamal is a lively, well-built man of 32, who prides himself on his muscular physique. When I met him, he was wearing shorts and singlet, looking like a sportsman who has just been jogging. His family came from Bihar two generations ago. They live in Kidderpore, where his father owns a small electrical business. His parents had become very insistent that he get married. Until now, he has been able to put off the day, arguing that he needs to complete his education, a project with which his parents have little sympathy. They are illiterate, pious and conservative, with no understanding of the need for, or indeed the value of, education. Kamal says, 'They think, what is the point of staying at school, when you can get economic security by working?'

I met Kamal in Minto Park, a small haven of green in the centre of Kolkata, although hemmed in by the by-pass, main roads, and overlooked by the white-painted structure of a private nursing home. There is a lake and a fountain with variegated lights that play on the surface of the water. It is a place where well-to-do families go for exercise, a safe environment where women in sarees and trainers stride out in the humid evening for long walks. It is also a discreet meeting-place for gay men. Kamal had worked in a chappal-factory, in a shopping mall and as a companion to an elderly widower, who gave him a modest sum of money before he died. With this, he had travelled, but since the money ran out, he has been 'looking around' for a relationship. He also needs to study and to work for his living, since he feels that, having grown up in an inward-looking Muslim community, he is ignorant and unfamiliar with the world. He has enrolled in a Bachelor of Commerce correspondence course, and is planning to learn IT skills.

These brief biographical details, however, give no account of the complexity and originality of his character. Vivacious and animated, he is highly intelligent and his lack of formal education has been supplemented by a self-taught comprehensive knowledge of the world. He has learned English (which he speaks fluently) from books, TV, magazines and newspapers, not from literature or academic study.

He is also looking for a father-figure. He met an American tourist in Kolkata who took him to five-star hotels, which he did not like. He took this friend to his home, but it was too humble for the American who was shocked by the poverty ('Actually, we are not poor'), and quickly fled.

> He will not come back to India. I think he found it not very comfortable, standards of cleanliness were not high enough for him. He didn't feel safe outside the comfort of five-star hotels. He now goes to Mexico for his holidays and has Mexican boy-friends.

Kamal's ideal is of elderly Western men. He mentioned how much he was attracted to former British Prime Minister John Major, but his idols are John Wayne and the older Cary Grant. He says, 'I don't like Indian men. They are too caught up with their wives and mothers and children and aunts and uncles and all the rest of the family relations to be able to make serious friendship with other men.'

He is not a devout Muslim, although he claims to be a believer. He wants to work in the social sector, for the good of humanity and the betterment of the poor. He is exasperated and unhappy with the poverty of ambition of so many of his Muslim peers in India. Kamal is a desperately hungry man, urgently seeking not only love and affection but also intellectual companionship and stimulus.

Kamal is disgusted by what he sees as the inertia, the dirt and grime of Indian cities, the inconsiderateness of people. He idealises the West, deploring an absence of a scientific bent of mind among Muslims in particular. The West is, to him, the future – progress – and although he recognises the advances India has made, he feels that he has been held back by his minority status (in more than one respect). He wants to be involved in 'modern education', although he left school after the tenth standard.

He knows he has no marketable skills. He feels alone, without a bosom-friend to unburden himself to, a stranger in his own culture. Indeed, he has re-made himself in the image of an imaginary West; a culturally displaced person, a strange social anomaly; he expresses his hatred of ostentation, excessive wealth and greed, but says he is also estranged from the poor people whose son he is.

He had a relationship with a teacher when he was adolescent, but it seems that no one perceived the potential in him or encouraged him to learn. 'One day at school, a teacher asked me why I was wearing a T-shirt with a picture on it. "That is a map of Latin America," I said. "And where is that?" the teacher sneered.' It seems from his teachers he learned about sex, but little more.

Later, he made a friendship with a man from the Netherlands and spent six months with him in his house near Rotterdam.

This man was a factory worker who had been forced to retire because of a heart condition. Kamal secured a visa for six months, and it was understood that at the end of that time he would have to leave. Kamal returned to India, even hungrier and more restless, unsettled by his glimpse of the paradise that is the West.

I asked Kamal about his religious faith and being gay. He saw no contradiction, since, he said, 'This is what I am. If Allah made me like this, how can I be otherwise?'

## VII
## AN ENLIGHTENED FATHER

At the end of a blind alley in Beniapukur, we called on Mohammad Jan-e-Alam. He was bathing in preparation for the evening prayer. He asked us to wait outside his house on a wooden bench that stood against a peeling yellow-washed wall beneath a line of washing. When he came out, he was wearing a long white kamiz and an Islamic topi, which did not cover his abundant black hair. He has lived here for 40 years. He is a modest man, who appeared puzzled that anyone should want to know what he thinks. He worked as a butcher in the Newmarket just behind Chowringhee in the centre of the city. His father was also a butcher. Mohammad Jan-e-Alam started work in his father's shop when he was 18 years old. His father never attended school and neither did he. Mohammad Jan-e-Alam was taught at home by a private religious teacher. He is a tall, gentle man, who was determined that his daughters should be educated as well as his sons. How many daughters do you have? He hesitated a moment, as though reluctant to say out of some residual shame at fathering many girls. It turns out he has seven daughters and three sons. All have been educated. Mohammad Jan-e-Alam's wife died 18 months ago. One son, a tailor, remains at home to look after his father. 'All the girls are married. Three of them studied to the tenth standard and four have academic degrees. I tried so hard to make sure they would not be disadvantaged in life. Three girls are teachers in local schools, and all of them give private tuitions.' Mohammad Jan-e-Alam is well known in the neighbourhood, and has inspired others to follow his example. A woman from the building where we are sitting, with a broad smile and kohl-darkened eyes, comes out to confirm what Mohammad Jan-e-Alam is saying. She, too, understands the value of women's education, in this case, her own. She has studied English, in order to be able to speak to her student son in English, because she wanted to help him, but also, she says, because there is nothing to stop women continuing life-long education. She is lucky because she knows that the education many women receive starts only after marriage, when they are given a crash course in the selfishness of men.

## VIII
## THE CHAPPAL FACTORY

In all of the Muslim areas of central Kolkata, ground-floor workshops where chappals are made stand open to the street. Mohammad Sayeed, barefoot, wearing a blue check lungi and white shirt, sits on a bamboo stool and, although he concentrates on his work, looks up constantly to exchange a few words with neighbours and passers-by. These streets are intensely convivial and, although they work incessantly, people still manage to monitor everything that happens. This is one reason why these poor communities are 'safe': morality is enforced by crowds.

People show no astonishment when asked about their business, their life, their religion. Mohammad Sayeed's grandfather came to Kolkata from Bihar 60 or 70 years ago. He has been doing this work for 15 years, despite having achieved his Higher School Certificate. He is obviously an intelligent man, and it seems he would have preferred to do something more challenging. When I asked him if he is disappointed with his work, he says, 'No, Allah is great, I thank Allah for what I have. How could I be disappointed?' But he still does not want his children to follow him in this labour.

Mohammad Sayeed gets orders from the wholesalers, buys the material in the market, and gives it to his workers to fulfill the commission. He employs four men. Business is not good at the moment. This is an understatement. For although chappals units are the most common manufacturing enterprise in the Muslim areas – there must be several hundred of them – they do not provide the secure livelihood they appear to. Chinese goods are available in the market, mass-produced imports which are cheaper than anything Kolkata can produce. Mohammad Sayeed's profit is between 5 per cent and 8 per cent. His workshop makes 50 pairs a day. He says, with a tinge of bitterness, 'We are not a business any more, we are labour.' In a single observation, he encapsulates the anxiety of people whose skills have been degraded. The wholesalers tell him which dealers he must go to for his materials, because there are unofficial agreements between wholesalers and their preferred merchants.

The soles of the sandals are cut out from a big square of rubber and the waste, the ribbons of material from which the ghostly footprints have been cut, is sold at 4 rupees per kilo. Mohammad Sayeed says retail shops make 100 per cent profit; but to set up a shop you need capital. This work is good for survival, but it does not provide enough to keep the family.

Mohammad Sayeed has a wife and six children, two boys and four girls. 'There is more supply than demand. Muslims have always been able to get work in the chappals trade, but this is no longer secure. The wholesalers' monopoly dictates where the manufacturer must buy, and this increases their profit at our expense. If there is any defect in the finished product, they reject it and withhold payment. Sometimes, they can be very critical, and you never know when a high proportion of your work is going to be thrown out.'

He has rooms, which he rents out at 300–400 rupees per month (about $8) to supplement his income. One room is set aside for his children's study. This property was a gift from his brother, who inherited it not from his parents but from the parents of his wife, Mohammad Sayeed's *phuphi*, their father's sister. His brother owns 26 rooms altogether.

Mohammad Sayeed can foresee a time when Chinese imports will displace large numbers of Muslim shoe-workers. The industry is not secure. Chinese rexine is already widely used, since its quality is better and the price lower than the Indian equivalent. It evokes a frightening possibility: the last thing the people here need is yet more unemployment. As it is, there are too many child workers and too many adults unemployed: a sure indicator of the downward pressure on prices. It adds yet another element of instability, waiting to undermine the fragile hold that Muslims have in the city economy.

IX

ALI

I spent a lot of time with Ali in his house, close to Mohammad Sayeed's workshop. Ali is 35, a highly intelligent school dropout, who has scavenged his education on the streets of Kolkata, a ragpicker of pedagogy. His family house is a tall, four-storey concrete building of which they are the theka tenants (holders of government-owned land). Built about 15 years ago, it is, of course, illegal. Money had to be paid to the local councillor before construction could begin. The staircases are dark and uneven, and in any case, it was obviously badly built, since large cracks are appearing in the concrete. At the top of the house, on the flat roof, there is a kind of street in the sky, *barsati* (rooftop) dwellings, a row of one-storey houses with red roof-tiles. Some of these are occupied by family members, others are tenants. This is characteristic of many theka tenancies: once their presence has been authorised by the government, they invest in building. Although illegal, the practice is so widespread that people imagine that they are safe from demolition by virtue of the sheer numbers who live in this way. In addition, there are tens of thousands of tenants who live in rented huts and rooms on the properties, so any large-scale clearance would be politically impossible.

This does not prevent selective condemnation of buildings by officials of the city corporation. Ali's family house is clearly unsafe, and they are trapped between fear of demolition and an unsaleable property. There is also a real risk that it might just collapse anyway.

Ali has a room on the roof, on a corner facing west and south. Two glassless windows: a warm evening wind inhabits the curtain which flaps, a persistent ghost tethered to a rail. The room is a concrete cube. There is a bed with cushions and a pile of blankets against the chill winter nights. No ornament relieves the plain interior. A small television set on a metal table, a calendar and a clock; an oval mirror in a broken frame and a few wisps of tinsel recalling some distant festival. There is a grille at one window, but the other stands open. Through it, you can see how the neighbourhood is changing. Originally, there were self-built huts. These were then replaced by kholabari houses – single storey, brick, with tiled roofs. Looking down, you can see the blood-red waves of rooftops, a muddy sea of blood. Many of these have now been replaced by new buildings; some apartment blocks are legal housing for the middle class. These threaten both the old houses and dilapidated and unauthorised buildings like this one. On the roof of Ali's building, unprotected by any fence, children are flying kites, rhomboids of yellow and turquoise tissue, an aerial geometry against a pale winter sky.

Hasna Khatoon, Ali's mother, is a woman in her late 60s, with silver-grey hair and a sweet expression. The family exemplifies the fate of many poor Muslims – a story of migration, acclimatisation to urban poverty, efforts to rise, setbacks and reverses that jeopardise every effort to make a safe, stable life. The only advantage of a condemned building, she says, is that they pay no tax to the Corporation. Why the building was inspected no one knows, unless it had been reported as an unsafe structure. 'If they wish, they can pull it down at any time.'

Her grandfather came to Kolkata long before Partition, from Golando in what is now Bangladesh. He worked for the municipality of Kolkata. Hasna Khatoon's father became a driver, whose work was to carry hunters – mostly British officials – into the forest to kill wild animals, which they did with reckless exuberance, starting many species, especially tigers, on the long road to extinction. In the house he had many horns, antlers and pelts of creatures his employers and their guests had killed.

Hasna Khatoon has four boys and five girls. Do you think of yourselves as poor? I asked. Ali says they are lower middle class; certainly not among the poorest, but people who are driven, because life is a constant effort not to fall back into misery. 'It seems sometimes that we are hanging on, that we are the hunted, always being chased by poverty. It snaps at our ankles, and if we stop running, it will catch us.'

His mother says,

> I am exhausted. My life is ended. Although my children work hard, they do not get sufficient pay. I have never seen good days. My mother's family came from Bihar. My mother's father was an educated person. I have done the best I could for my family. I married off all my daughters, but three of them came back. A mother is not supposed to look after her daughters.

Hasna Khatoon feels, in some way, she is culpable for the failure of her daughters' marriage.

When Ali recounts his own story and that of his family, it is from another perspective. 'My father was a bookbinder. Our parents had nine children, so my father's income could never match his needs. They sent us to work in nearby chappal-making units. I started when I was six or seven.' Ali's first job was cleaning the adhesive that had stuck to the chappals, and he was paid 3 rupees per week (about 6 US cents).

> I had to go from one workshop to another, carrying materials and finished merchandise. The family was in financial crisis, there was no

money to spend on education. By the age of eight, I was working in a paint-shop. I used to climb the ladder to take down the different colours. That was when I first started to learn English – I learned names of the colours first. The shop was in Beckbagan, not far from here. I also went as a small boy as a servant in someone's house. That lady was kind, and she taught me the English ABC.

Later, my mother sent me to a garage to become an apprentice. I was very keen to work with the senior mechanic, and when he accepted me I felt such euphoria I went wild with joy, and in my enthusiasm I tried to jump over a wire with which they were testing car parts. I tripped and broke my hand. I broke it three times, because I loved playing football. That career was finished before it started. By the age of 14, I was selling newspapers on the street. It was a miserable time. We lived in a one-storey house then, before the building was made. We had bedbugs. My mother briefly sent me to school: I went to a madrasa for two years, but then I had to leave because we needed more income. I went selling Phenyl cleaning fluid door to door.

I got a scholarship through a Muslim organisation, and was admitted to a typing and shorthand course. I couldn't keep it up, because at home we had no light for studying, and in the morning there was no food. I started work again, this time in a bill deposit centre, where people go to pay electricity and water bills, and for a small sum, the centre delivers the money to the company.

It makes me sad when I think about it, that I never really had an opportunity to develop. My nephew goes with his father to the chappal workshop when he finishes school. His father gives him 10 rupees per day for the work he does. It reminds me of how I was, except that I worked full-time from when I was very small.

My parents were pious, but our circumstances were wretched. We needed income to feed the family. Hunger cannot wait. I have had 32 different jobs, I can't remember them all. I taught myself English from books and later from TV. I found refuge at last in teaching. Although I had no qualification and no experience, I set up a blackboard and held English-language classes. I also published a crudely xeroxed magazine for young people, which I distributed to children at schools in the neighbourhood. English was like Greek to all the people around me; it was only the privileged who had access to English-medium instruction. I realised later that it was social action that attracted me. But I was proud that, as a Class II dropout, I still managed to outmatch the people who went to posh schools. I don't know how. I sleep and dream in English, I always had a love for the language. I am still groping in the dark to find something I can commit myself to. I am employed at Tiljala-SHED as a driver, although in reality my duties go far beyond my job description.

My father died because we had no money for the medicine he needed. He was suffering from diabetes. It could have been treated. He had a coating of white in his mouth, it choked him and he couldn't talk or eat. It was very painful. We knew he was dying and just had to watch him die. That is one of the most bitter things for the poor – to know that medicine and care are available, but to know also that these things are beyond their reach.

I used to sleep on the roadside near our house, because the room we had was very small – eight by ten – for eleven people. We lived a cramped life, and there was no privacy. The hut was one storey with a little land. We were its owners, because it had been built by my grandfather. He and my grandmother had two sons and two daughters. Two of these had no children, so the property was left to my father and my aunt.

After he died, my mother made it into a three-storey building. The contractor cheated us. He made our lives hell. My mother had no money to fight them. She was lured into a contract, and the construction was cheap and unreliable. I could not comfort her. On this, my grandfather's property, we had several rooms on rent, but they were good for nothing and the rent was maintained artificially low by the government, who were on the side of the tenants for political reasons. By the time we commissioned the contractor to make the building, he was supported by the *goondas* [thugs] and toughs of the CPI(M). I was too young then to understand the complexity of what was going on. I know now.

When the government took over the land, we became the theka tenants. We were not supposed to construct, but the political parties said 'Just build anyway', because they were getting money from the contractors. My brother is a member of the Party. I stayed away from politics. I just wanted to be a social worker.

My four sisters got married. We had to find money for the dowry. Two marriages didn't work out; and the child of one other sister has a hole in her heart. One sister realised on the day after she got married that she had made a wrong match. She was married off in a hurry; because in our culture, keeping daughters at home is seen as a problem. She wasn't willing to stay with her husband. She is now 26. She couldn't handle life and didn't know what to do. One other was married and went to Haryana. She came back sick. Three times she came home. She became depressed and unhappy; we didn't know she had been physically ill-treated. She now lives with her husband in one of the rooms on the roof. It was the husband's mother who had tormented her. They have three children.

My third sister has six daughters, but her husband drinks. He comes and abuses her every couple of weeks. He lives in Kolkata. My brothers work in chappal factories. They cannot fight for my sisters, so that duty also falls to me. And then my job is not secure. There is never enough money.

My big brother married independently. He had a difference with his wife and went away to Mumbai with his daughter. He worked in a chappals factory in Mumbai. He returned home, and he now wants to teach us about life. Because he has been out of Kolkata, he thinks he has seen and understood the world.

Ali is a perceptive and sensitive man, marginalised by society, excluded from education and compelled to work at a level far below his competence. In this way, he has become truly radical; questioning, open and alert to the absurdities of society and the world; but torn, because he is also profoundly committed to his family, for which he feels he is now responsible. His position has bestowed upon him rare insight and understanding. He has been unable to marry – a serious disability in the culture. He fell in love with a Japanese girl who came to work as an intern at Tiljala-SHED. The feeling was mutual. She stayed with the family and adapted well to the crowded household, who took her to their hearts. She wants Ali to go into business to earn money and perhaps join her in Japan. He is highly conscious of the conflict between desire and duty, inclination and the impossibility of abandoning so many people who, in one way or another, depend upon him.

# 4
# Defining Slums

The use of the word 'slum' is misleading. It has come in for much criticism recently, and rightly so. It is a concept borrowed from the streets and tenements of nineteenth-century Britain. The word contains an assumption that the orderly improvement to urban landscapes witnessed in Britain will eventually extend to the places of savage destitution to be found all over the 'developing' world. (This is another thoughtless word: all societies are developing. The word 'developed' has determinist implications.) It is false to transfer words from other cultures to describe the habitations of the contemporary poor.

Most definitions of slums are restricted to the physical conditions rather than the social relationships within them. 50 years ago, UNESCO suggested a slum was 'a building, group of buildings or an area characterised by overcrowding, deterioration, insanitary conditions, an absence of facilities or amenities which, because of these conditions or any of them, endanger the health, safety or morals of its inhabitants or the community.' A later attempt by UN-Habitat to define a slum household listed five amenities, the absence of any one of which would indicate such a household: access to an improved water supply, that is, which was sufficient, affordable and the procuring of which did not involve excessive effort; improved sanitation, that is, a system of disposal of waste, and a toilet shared by a 'reasonable' number of people; security of tenure, documents demonstrating people's right to live in the property they occupy, protected from eviction; durability of housing, a habitation of permanent and adequate structure; sufficient living room, which means not more than two people to a room.[10]

The emphasis is on the material living conditions; but many have argued, among them Dr M. K. A. Siddiqui,[11] that equally important in the evaluation of slum neighbourhoods is the quality of interaction and support between people. In some of the most desolate places a sense of shared predicament and mutuality mitigates some of the harshness of living. This is, of course, no argument in favour of the wretched circumstances in which 1 billion people on earth now live; but levels of hostility and distrust between people may exacerbate the misery of circumstances which are not necessarily, at first sight, particularly poor. This offers a clue as to why some of the poorest housing in the West, although incomparably better than that of the poor of Kolkata or Dhaka, most certainly qualifies as slums. One of the most touching aspects of Kolkata's Muslim communities is people's hospitable spirit, their readiness to offer part of their meagre resources to those in even greater need than they are, since they know there is always someone worse off than they are; and that tomorrow, given the threats and hazards of daily life, they too may also be in need of the charitable impulses of others.

I

## THE POOR HAVE NO BIOGRAPHY

Just as the slum is believed to have no history, so the poor have no biography. A few sparse details sketch out their existence, usually illustrative of their 'plight' – a story of land forfeited through debt, river erosion or distress sale, so the people came to the city to live on the pavement, to become maidservants or to work as rickshaw drivers. Their loves and sorrows are eclipsed by their social condition, epic stories resumed in laconic reports by journalists, academics or non-government organisation social workers, and often referred to by television presenters as 'these people' who, more often than not have lost everything; evicted or ousted, often in the name of 'development'. If they are also Muslim, even these brief descriptions of misery are overtaken by demands that they state whether or not they support the work of terrorists.

The 'urban poor' are, however, often invoked by politicians and policy makers as a semi-abstract entity for whom something must be done. That something is usually connected with their disappearance. In 2009 the President of India announced that the country would be 'slum-free' within five years. The most effective way of achieving this is already well-known to city authorities. This is to reduce the land area on which the poor live. Poor people in the city are being subject to a process of *compression*. In Kolkata, it is estimated that the poor now occupy a decreasing proportion of the city's land: in 1997, of the 187.33 square kilometres within the city limits, 21.35 square kilometres were slum areas, in which just under 50 per cent of the population lived, that is, on less than 10 per cent of the land.[12] Nothing suggests that since then the poor have gained ground, except numerically; and indeed, one of the most obvious aspects of contemporary Kolkata is the erection of hectares of densely-packed skyscrapers, which are represented by idealised artists' impressions of their final form – lawns, flowers and landscapes with names like Lakeview, Mayfair or Berkeley Towers; a projection often far removed from the finished reality. (Mumbai has achieved an even greater feat of constriction: 6 per cent of the city land now houses 60 per cent of the people.)

But poor settlements and the communities which grow out of them have a past, as do the people who live here. The policy of the Calcutta Improvement Trust was one of consistent eviction from the early twentieth century until the 1960s. The CIT demolished slums and redistributed land to the business community. Many of those now living on the edge of the commercial centre of the city are the descendants of those whose labour actually erected the grand buildings around Chowringhee, for the sake of which they were evicted. The labouring poor settled in areas formerly on the outskirts of Calcutta (as the city was historically known), *bagans* or garden estates, on which the owners originally built accommodation for their own workers. This accounts for the backwardness of slum areas, since, apart from institutionalised discrimination, the conditions are also a result of the system of land tenure which governs them, a survival of the old *zamindari* system. Theka tenancy (which means a contract for temporary possession) arose in colonial Calcutta, whereby landlords rented out large parcels of their garden estates, mainly to their own employees, who in turn, built huts on the plots and rented them out to migrants, workers and families. These 'gardens' were more intensively built up and became overcrowded and insanitary quarters for the poor. A three-tier system developed: landlords (who lived elsewhere), the hut-owners (the so-called theka tenants) and the families or individuals who rented a single room from them. The Theka Tenancy Act was amended in 1949, to give greater security to those renting from the theka tenants. These were forbidden to construct *pakka* buildings, so the owners had no incentive to improve the property.

In 1981, the Theka Tenancy Act drastically curbed the power of private landlords, since the state took over ownership of the land, indeed became the zamindar of the slum areas. Today, government is the landlord, with, beneath them the 'hut-owners' (theka tenants) and then the tenants. The word hut-owner is misleading. A hut may involve ten or twelve rooms, organised around a courtyard or in a row, usually erected on land acquired by earlier migrants who had prospered in the complex division of labour created by the growth and spread of Kolkata.

# 5

# Tiljala Road

Tiljala Road is one of the most extensive of the approximately 5000 'slums' in Kolkata, of which some 3000 are 'authorised' or recognised as legal. Following the Act of 1981, by which the government assumed ownership of the land, Tiljala Road was provided with water, electricity and some sanitary improvements. It benefited also from a World Bank-funded Bustee Improvement Programme, which regenerated many settlements on the verge of collapse through a combination of neglect and an absence of basic facilities. Since the improvements of that time, Tiljala has grown, both by natural increase from within, and also by the migration of relatives and neighbours of those already here. The services provided a quarter of a century ago have long been overwhelmed, and function badly or not at all.

Tiljala Road settlement is bisected by the railway line that leads to the nearby station of Park Circus. Part of the area – owned by the railway authority – remains illegally occupied. Trains pass by every few minutes, rattling the fragile habitations that stand within a metre of the line. This whole area is part of an arc of mainly Muslim settlements, bounded by the Muslim cemeteries, the overgrown village that was old Ballygunge and the more squalid areas of Topsia and Tangra, and stretching beyond Park Circus into Beniapukur.

The railway line is a main pathway for pedestrians, vendors and hawkers, who sell guavas, oranges, aubergines, onions or cauliflower on the concrete platform. Accidents are common, but most people have learned to adapt to the presence of the great Indian Railways engines that share their living-space – a kind of mechanised urban equivalent of buffaloes in the rural areas – and rattle, day and night, through the neighbourhood. In spite of this uneasy co-existence, you do not have to go far to find people who have lost limbs in railway accidents.

The official market, which starts under the bridge where the Tiljala Road settlement begins, is on railway land, where a plaque announces that 'an eviction stay order until further notice' was issued by the court in 1997. These stalls provide shelter against the sun and rain, and the reprieve of 13 years ago has given them a provisional stability (which says a great deal in these conditional and volatile communities). In the meantime, a committee of stallholders has been set up to recommend improvements. Mohammad Ashraf, who wears a blue lungi, Islamic topi and grey beard, has been a trader here for 40 years. He makes a daily profit of between 100 and 150 rupees, selling onions with red papery skins, opalescent garlic, pyramids of earth-smelling potatoes and scarlet chillies. He believes the market traders will be very happy if the railway adopts them, since they have been negotiating with the railway authorities for many years to establish themselves as legal tenants. In spite of the traders' persistence, the fear is never quite dispelled that the Railway may dislodge them, since the price of land continues to rise. If this should happen, they will be forced out onto the spaces beside the railway track, where the small – mainly women – traders sit, with their inferior, more limited merchandise. The women occupy every available piece of ground; sitting

on heaps of grey stone railway chippings, against the wall of
the Missionaries of Charity hospice, at the edge of the station
and in the constricted gaps between the up and down track.

## I
## LEGALITY AND ILLEGALITY

The market offers for sale goods that would be thrown away
in Europe: a woman sells nothing but chicken claws, which
look like clusters of scaly yellow scorpions. The innards of
goats – lights, livers and stomach – are spread on plastic
trays, while crimson and wax-white shanks hang from curved
hooks, and a triangular head, sliced in half, looks both ways
with its vigilant glazed eyes. Another stall sells goat-tails –
thin, with wiry hair and virtually meatless. At another trestle,
a little girl of about eight is shaking a rag tied to a bamboo
cane, with which she ineffectually whisks at the flies. These
do not move, since most of them are anchored fast in the
melting green sweetness of cakes.

The least profitable market vendors sit or squat on the
ground, with their frugal goods spread on a length of plastic
or jute. Mehrun Bewa leans against a green-painted wall
belonging to the railway, her arm resting on a raised knee.
She left her job as maidservant to start her small 'business'
– selling tablets of Lux and Pioneer soap, sponges, silver
metal pot-scourers, toothbrushes, washing powder. She
took a loan of 1000 rupees to invest after her husband died,
and this provides an income of 50–60 rupees per day. Her
ten-year-old son is an 'apprentice' in a chappals factory.
She lives on railway land and so pays no rent, but knows
she can be evicted at any time. She buys her merchandise

from a manufacturing unit and wholesaler; they will take back any unsold goods. She pays nothing for her spot by the railway track, but it is, she says, like everything else she does, illegal. Mehrun Bewa's family came from Bihar when she was a child: illegal, unauthorised, prohibited, disallowed, forbidden, unlawful – the lives of the poor exist in a condition of transgressive suspension, from which it is such a small step to the denial of their rights as citizens.

The dividing line between 'authorised' and 'unauthorised' settlements is arbitrary. 'How can we be encroachers,' people ask, 'in our own land?' Many spoke of having been evicted by poverty, as though it were a person; and it is indeed embodied in the individuals who come to move them on, to eject or banish them – police, landlords, officials. One young Muslim activist said:

> We are made illegitimate in many ways. We are given to understand that India is not our homeland, so we are already made to feel we are in an alien country. Then we are called 'squatters', which means we have no right to remain where we are. Our presence is 'illegal'. How can any human being be illegal? Who has to ask permission to be born? I came into the world as a trespasser. It is easy for the police, politicians or the army to eliminate us, because we barely exist in the first place.

Next to Mehrun Bewa sits Sitara Begum, who has been selling second-hand clothes here for the past three years. Her husband is a rickshaw-puller, earning 100–150 rupees ($2–3) per day, while she makes 80–90 rupees ($2). Sitara Begum buys second-hand clothes near the Ram Mandir in College Street in the city centre, and makes 30–40 per cent profit on each piece she sells. She has lived in Kolkata all her life, but her family came from Pakistan at Partition – a curious reverse migration which she did not explain. Her father was a driver. She still has relatives in Karachi. Her children are with her husband's family in Bangalore, where they go to school – an unusual dispersal, even by the migratory standards of contemporary India. She lives in a single-room house in Tiljala with her husband, her husband's sister and her husband. Sitara Begum works from 8 until 2. She points to some of the items on display – an orange shirt which she bought for ten rupees and will sell for 20; a blouse, bought for 15 rupees, on sale at 25. Sometimes, she pays a child to sweep the space where she sets out her display clean of dust. The house is cheap, a rent of 50 rupees per month, and they pay 200 for electricity. She sits under a battered red umbrella, which casts its theatrical pink light onto her face and saree.


## II
## THE REFORMED ADDICT

Salim is seated cross-legged on a trestle beneath a broad golf umbrella, selling cold drinks of yogurt and water. The yogurt is kept fresh in a zinc bucket next to a box of ice, which is melting rapidly in the growing warmth of the day. Salim was born in Tiljala, although his family came many years ago from Bihar. He believes Tiljala was a far worse place to live then than now. He took drugs as a youth. He was idle and vain as a teenager.

> I did no work. I used to take hallucinogenic drugs. My mind was always in the clouds. It was as if my real life was always somewhere else. I lived a life of chaos, in which anything could happen. I took brown sugar and injections of Nurofen and tuberculosis vaccine. That gives

you a high like nothing else. I used to feed my habit by snatching
chains and purses. I used to threaten people with a knife.

Salim is now 42. His teenage son Irshad, stands listening
to his father. He is more interested in getting high through
education than through drugs.

Salim has four children, a girl of 18 about to be married,
and two younger children at school. 'How did you get away
from drugs before they destroyed you?' He says, 'I started
to hate myself. I realised that my life would be a wasteland
if I didn't take control. I was not stupid, although I did not
have a proper education.' He makes his renunciation of drugs
appear easy. Was it really his willpower, or was it the love of
his parents, maturity, marriage and children that drew him
from his addictions? He said some people are unable to give
it up, because drugs have seized hold of them like evil spirits.
For him, it was a habit, a choice which he was able to alter,
because he never really surrendered his soul to it.

Salim pays no rent for the stall, and makes 200 rupees profit
per day. The rent for his one-room house is 200 rupees per
month and they pay 400 for electricity. As we are leaving,
he offers us a *bel* fruit as a gift, a kind of outsized grapefruit.


III

THE CHORUS OF MARKET WOMEN

Along the peeling ochre wall of the Missionaries of Charity,
the market women who are mainly vegetable vendors sit at
intervals of a couple of metres or so. Vigilant, entreating
customers, they also constitute a kind of chorus – a continuous
lament and observation, a commentary on poverty and the

misfortunes of women. They have bought their produce in the wholesale market and sit all day for a profit of 50–60 rupees (about $1.30): small quantities of purple aubergines, foamy cauliflower, the emerald corrugation of ridged gourd, ripening tomatoes, green peas and dark bundles of spinach. They buy the goods on credit and pay for the produce at the end of a day's work, which may be prolonged if there are no customers, since the traders do not take back unsold goods. The women complain that, although they have taken loans for microcredit, the investment scarcely pays, and in any case there are always more urgent calls upon the money – a daughter's heart operation, a dowry, replacement for goods destroyed in a fire. They sit. But they are also watchful, and little escapes their critical gaze: they serve as an informal community police, knowing all irregularities of behaviour, an illicit word here, a flirtation there, a piece of insolence, an indecent look. Juleka Bibi, Asma Bibi, their husbands old, retired, unfit or simply unable to find work, are the principal agents of family survival. Asma Bibi bewails her fate, that she has five daughters and only one son, and he is handicapped. He is paralysed in his left arm, although he works, collecting old paint tins that will be sold to the toymakers to be turned into drums. The women also have their own strategies for selling yesterday's leftovers, which they mix with fresh vegetables, bunching the spinach tightly together so that the wilted leaves disappear in the fresh outer ones. How can we send our children to school, without resources? What kind of life is this, to sit here selling food, when we have not enough to feed our own families? The stories merge, the universal complaint of the poor – how shall we bring up a new generation in safety, how will our children resist the temptations of poverty – drugs and crime for boys, the easy money of prostitution for girls, how shall we bear the sorrow of knowing that their future will be no better, and may be worse, than our own? Where shall we find peace this side of the grave?

The men do not give voice to the epic lament of women, who at least have the relief of articulating their sense of injustice. If men appear more stoical and less likely to talk of the afflictions of adversity, this is, perhaps, also because they are protected by women, sheltered by their ingenuity and ability to produce something out of nothing, to provide solace, to mitigate the cruelties of life, to still the crying of children and assuage the discontent of adolescents. It is the energy of women that drives poor communities. This is a secret against which men, for their own pride and sense of self, must be shielded; it is a sad hypocrisy, this sweet collusion of women, who must also protect their men against the obvious – their own powerlessness in the world.

It is not that men do not suffer. In all poor areas, there is a high incidence of disability, as a result of injury, accident or sickness. Ajay works in a chappals unit opposite the wall against which the women sell vegetables. He is one of eight young men, working with rapt concentration on the pile of finished yellow-and-black rexine and rubber chappals. Ajay – one of the few Hindus in the community – is handicapped. His legs were severed just above the knee by a train accident on the line running into Park Circus station. He was then a teenager. How did the accident happen? He is vague, and says the daring of the young sometimes ends in disaster. Adolescent boys often do things as a dare, risking their lives to prove they are without fear, to show, perhaps, their belief in their own invulnerability, that pitiable inheritance of male illusion.

Ajay has three brothers and one sister, now married. He studied until Class VIII. His father is dead and his mother stays at home. Ajay earns 100–150 rupees per day. He is the only earning member of the family; this is a common expression which scarcely indicates the awful responsibility this imposes, since it is only the strength and earning power of a single individual that stands between them and absolute destitution. Ajay regrets he cannot run his family on this income. They pay rent of 450 rupees per month and electricity is about 250. He cuts the soles for the chappals, twelve hours a day. He lives nearby, and travels on a small cart he made himself, with wheels, which he propels by chappals worn on his hands. Ajay gives me his mobile number, and asks me to call. I said I would, but did not.

## IV

### MODERNISED POVERTY

We passed from the street into the ground floor of a concrete building, already stained by monsoon rain. The outside – which is an anonymous, fairly recent structure – gives no idea of the conditions within. It is quite dark, a cavernous entry, with a flight of steps which protrudes onto the concrete, a hazard to anyone who does not know the building; although there can be few chance visitors to this sombre location. Here is evidence that even those who no longer live in the rough self-built huts and shanties are not necessarily better off. As our eyes adjusted to the darkness, we made our way to the end of the corridor, where we faced two doors. The entrance on the right opened into a small high room with no window and no ventilation, about eight feet by ten. There was a single

low-energy light bulb high up on the wall, which shed a pale
lustre onto the gloomy scene beneath, the walls, once blue,
dimmed now by metallic dust.

Sheikh Sona lives and works here with his wife. He was
born in Tiljala Road, and this airless brick box is where he
sleeps, eats and labours. It is like entering a prison cell, a
place of incarceration for the supreme crime of being poor.
Sheikh Sona, his wife and son are all working on what looks
like a kind of make-work, almost invisible in the vast division
of labour of the world. They are glazing clips for pens, the
metal holder by which pens may be attached to shirt or coat
pockets. The room is full of these metal objects which, when
they arrive, are tarnished and have jagged edges. Sheikh Sona
has a machine – rented from the manufacturer – into which he
fits a row of 20 or 30 clips. These are then fed into the mouth
of the machine, which abrades and polishes, at the same time
emitting a deadly cloud of tiny metallic particles. These hang
in the air before settling on any available surface – the rough
brick which juts unevenly into the room, the floor, ceiling fan
and bedding, and the hair, eyelashes and skin of the people.
Sheikh Sona collects the clips from a wholesaler in Canning
Street in the city centre and brings them here. The family
earn 1 rupee for every twelve dozen clips polished. There is
a deduction for the use of the machine.

The daily profit is between 150 and 200 rupees, although
work depends upon the level of orders received by the
manufacturer. It is extraordinary that it can be profitable
to the manufacturer to give out this work as home labour.

Sheikh Sona's son, Sheikh Nasir, is 25. He is married with
a four-year-old daughter. They sleep in a separate room in
the building, but Sheikh Sona and his wife have no other
retreat. For 18 years Sheikh Sona was working for another

master, and he decided only a few months earlier to start up on his own. Because he is now the owner, he must work harder: self-exploitation can be even more severe than when it is imposed by others. None of the family wears protective clothing. They are inhaling metal dust for up to ten hours a day. They are acutely conscious of their situation: 'By eating poison we earn our bread.' Sheikh Sona is 55; both he and his wife suffer from stomach problems and have difficulty breathing. There is no running water. He pays 50 rupees for the room, and 220 for electricity, most of which is consumed by the motor of the polishing machine.

On the left hand side of Sheikh Sona's room, a narrow concrete corridor opens into a diminutive bathroom, about three feet square, with a single faucet. From this constricted space you turn left into a dark shrunken room, lit only by a metal grille above head level. A bed takes up two-thirds of the narrow chamber and the only way to reach the bed is from the bottom, since it is bounded by concrete walls on either side. On it, a boy covered with blankets lies shivering with fever. He is one of the six children of Nasima Begum. In the space that remains she keeps her cooking pots, and clothes are stored in a glass-and-wood fronted almirah. When she is squatting by the cooking fire, there is no room for anyone to come and go. Nasima Begum's family migrated from Bihar long ago. Her husband works as chappal-maker for 500 rupees per week. They pay 50 rupees rent and about 500 for electricity for the light and the fan. There is a dusty TV set on a shelf above the kitchen-space. Just above my head there is another ledge, scarcely 30 centimetres wide and unprotected. Incredibly, two adolescent boys sleep here. To reach it, they climb an iron ladder fixed to the wall. Nasima Begum says they suffer constantly from waterborne diseases

– stomach pains, diarrhoea, malaria and typhoid. Two boys were studying at Don Bosco school, but they had to drop out after Class VIII and Class V respectively. Sheikh Yusuf, almost 18, is continuing his studies at the free night school. He would have preferred to continue at school, but he had to help with the family income. He is an 'apprentice', a helper to his father. His father takes a contract from the supplier and he subcontracts the work to the rest of the family. Sheikh Yusuf speaks a polite, correct English. His desire to learn is so intense, it vibrates, a living presence in the dark cavity that is home to eight people.

Are these blighted cells traps set by modernity for the people, the future of poverty in Kolkata, and the other cities of India? Flimsy huts of bamboo, associated with recent migration and precarious shelter, are swept away; even the makeshift tin-and-brick shanties are being cleared. If poverty is stacked vertically in concrete towers, it will not cease to be poverty; and if this has the advantage of making the poor invisible to the tender sensibility of the rich, it is of small benefit to them.

## V

### THE MENACE OF 'DEVELOPMENT'

The light is dazzling when we emerge from this unofficial prison visit. On the edge of a small dusty square, women have come out to prepare vegetables and to talk. Some boys are playing cricket, others football, so that the games overlap and the football hits the wickets and the cricket-ball flies over the stones representing the goal. Between concrete posts, sagging electricity lines (most of them illegal connections) form thick bands of black rubber.

We look back at the building we have just visited, which betrays nothing of the dark secrets it conceals. It is owned by a local CPI(M) leader. It is, perhaps no accident that his tenants should dwell in darkness, since the lights of an ideology that was to have illuminated the lives of the poor have long been extinguished.

The government had promised to remodel the slums. The Housing Development Corporation would build flats, and if the Kolkata authorities agreed to stand as guarantor, some could be sold to the better off while the rest could be cross-subsidised to provide better housing for tenants of dilapidated and unfit houses. But the city officials need money. The promoters need money. The police need money. These needs, which weigh more than the featherlight needs of the people, come together to create illegal constructions which profit everyone except those who have no home. If the government had been accountable, it would have ensured that the promoters provided homes for the tenants.

Overlooking the little square is a recently finished (illegal) block, four storeys high, which, early in 2010, sell at the rate of 70,000–80,000 rupees for 100 square feet (about $1500). Most of these are sold off to lower-middle class people, who have been able to accumulate just enough to gain a foothold in the housing market.

The hut-owner – that is, the owner of the properties on a parcel of land, the theka tenant – makes an illegal contract with the promoter. The owner is obliged by law to re-house the tenants on the ground floor at the same rent. There are, of course, ways around this. The rooms that replace the original huts are often smaller and pressure is often brought to bear upon tenants to 'encourage' them to move, so that their room can be sold on at a considerable profit. The owner will also get one or two flats in payment. The promoter sells the rest of the apartments, flats or rooms. Some of these are small – 100 square feet – while others are spread over 200 or 500 square feet. This particular new construction is very roughly built, with brick the colour of dried blood. The mortar has been carelessly applied, and protrudes in rough layers from the brickwork. There is no guarantee that it is structurally safe. The promoters often do not finish the work properly, but quickly vanish with the profit they have made. The government claims to know nothing about such transactions, and say that if they demolish illegal buildings, it is the occupants who will suffer.

But this is how poverty and insecurity mutate. Nothing remains still in the permanent upheaval known as development. During the 60 or more years that Tiljala Road has been occupied, original *kacha* huts of wood and bamboo were replaced by sturdier buildings of brick, concrete and corrugated metal. The legality or otherwise of these structures is one thing: their de facto existence, occupied by a population of perhaps a quarter of a million people, gives them an air of permanence. Some of the huts form single-storey lanes, following ancient walkways. The houses are small and overcrowded, so that life spills out onto narrow public spaces, where people sit, prepare vegetables, cook on clay chulhas, bathe and feed their children, pursue a livelihood and tell one another stories of survival and loss.

The threat to the settlement now comes not so much from increased population, lack of adequate employment, poor facilities and continuing poverty – although all of these continue to scar the lives of many of the inhabitants – but from these brick structures, appearing everywhere, rising above the rooftops of the old irregular housing clusters.

The *Telegraph* newspaper reported in 2005 that,

> around 10,000 acres of slum land in prime pockets are lying locked because of their peculiar legal status. Following the enactment of the Theka Tenancy Act, 1981, neither the state government nor the Calcutta (sic) Municipal Corporation has been able to take any meaningful step to develop the slum areas. Reason: the Act does not bestow the title of right to the precious acres on any individual or organisation. Officials of the government and the civic body have put their heads together to discuss how to free the plots and build housing estates for the middle and upper-middle classes on them. The proceeds from developing the land would be used for arranging alternative accommodation for the over five lakh families occupying the prime plots.[13]

The language is significant. The lands are 'locked'. These are 'precious acres'. 'Meaningful development' for the upper-middle classes is stalled. How the 'proceeds' could conceivably be spent on providing accommodation for the 2 million people currently occupying the degraded inner area of Kolkata is difficult to imagine. The discussion suggests further displacement, as well as greater confinement, of poor people.

It was reported early in 2008 that the West Bengal Land Minister had agreed to a plan to allow multi-storey building on theka tenancy land, provided that the tenants agreed to it. This does not appear to have entered into law, but on the ground, the process is already far advanced. Land values here, close to the downtown business area of Kolkata, are increasing. But since the government is the owner of the land, most of the new building is illegal, and adds further to an overloaded and barely functioning infrastructure.

Promoters and theka tenants collude to sell off rooms in the new buildings: the builder takes the *salami* (deposit, or 'good will money') paid in advance by the occupants of the new buildings and receives instalments of the agreed sum from them for an agreed number of years after completion. Those who occupy the new structures must close their eyes to the illegality of their new home, and are undeterred by the likelihood that the day will soon come when the municipality decides that big money is to be made out of selling land to large-scale developers. Newcomers to Tiljala Road are mainly those who have made just enough money, either through some small enterprise or working in the Gulf, to afford something slightly better than the cramped quarters of their neighbours.

## VI
## MOHAMMAD ALAMGIR: A LIFE IN TILJALA

Tiljala Road is more than 90 per cent Muslim, a communalising of urban poverty which has a long history in Kolkata, as well as in India more generally. Mohammad Alamgir was born and has spent most of his life here. He has recorded its story and monitored the changing nature of poverty in urban settlements. Now in his mid-50s, he has done everything possible to mitigate some of the worst injustices, to humanise what were some of the most degrading living conditions in the city and raise the horizons of poor Muslims. He is torn between pride in his achievement and a recognition of how much remains to be done, since improvements often have unintended consequences and are accompanied by unforeseen hazards.

His parents sold their small piece of land in Bihar and migrated to Kolkata at the time of Independence. Mohammad Alamgir's father sold meat door to door in the slum: the small shop where he worked is now a coaching centre for girls. Both Alamgir and his brother started work as children, he in a tailoring shop, his brother in a leather factory. The house where they lived as children is now a shoe-factory, where a dozen or more men and boys are employed. Tiljala was an area of leather-workers, which produced high quality goods – shoes, handbags and wallets – which were exported to Eastern Europe and the Soviet Union. With the collapse of Communism in Europe, this trade was wiped out – an early effect of globalisation; and in any case, many polluting tanning and leather industries were subsequently moved away from the central area of the city. Mohammad Alamgir continued his education, thanks to the charitable help of a family friend; and he went on to qualify as a teacher, social worker and later, as a lawyer. Education seemed the key to the uplift of the people; and he started a small voluntary school, which was recognised by government and incorporated into the official system in 1982.

Mohammad Alamgir's parents loved him dearly, but they did not understand the importance of education:

They never discussed it. They assumed that since they had been day-labourers from childhood, their children would continue like that. They were good people. My father was a very gentle man, a socialist. I had this sense of injustice from him. I remember aged people, mothers, sick people would go to my father to seek advice on marriages or disputes. I remember him sitting on a *charpai*, while deserted women, working mothers, widows came to him. I think I inherited this from him. He was recognised in the community as an intelligent man, illiterate, but accessible, knowledgeable and responsive to the sufferings of people.

Mohammad Alamgir evokes Tiljala Road as it was, when it remained a warren of provisional kacha houses:

Every morning you could not breathe for the cooking smoke. The kitchen was not separate, there was no ventilation, nothing. We had a charpai and a paraffin lamp, which also smelled very bad. It was impossible to learn or study. The school, too, provided no good teaching. The teachers didn't teach. Instead, they suggested you should join their tuition classes, where they would give you the education you were supposed to get at school. Instead of doing their job, they ran a private tuitions business.

Mohammad Alamgir has worked for a lifetime, improving the conditions the residents of Tiljala Road. His work illuminates both the possibilities and the limitations of non-government organisations. They can further the interests of the most disadvantaged groups – street-children, rag-pickers, widows, deserted women, the unemployed – but they cannot alter the onward march of the market economy, the appetite for land of the middle class, the obliteration of livelihoods by changing technologies, the effects of one-party rule for more than three decades. Non-government organisations have come in for a great deal of criticism in recent years, not least because they assumed an heroic role (particularly with the decay of socialism), and made grandiose claims about their transformative power. It seems they inherited some of the rhetoric abandoned by the Left. When it proves impossible for them to achieve what they have promised, they are reviled for their overblown rhetoric and exaggerated sense of power.

It is not that improvements to which non-government organisations have contributed are illusory: but in the context in which these are realised, they are easily transformed or mis-shapen by a system whose need for gain must take precedence over the need of vulnerable people. Poverty is indestructible, a bit like the cockroaches which infest every house, and capable of surviving all attempts to eliminate them.

The limits of the non-government organisation are also determined by political power in the neighbourhood. When a non-government organisation makes an effort to get a widow's pension, the official entitlements of old age, legal aid or any other statutory provision, they are told that 'no new cases are accepted', since resources have run out, been diverted or have otherwise become unavailable to those for whom they are, in theory, intended.

## VII
## THE WORKERS OF TILJALA ROAD

Tiljala Road is a place of relentless economic activity. Although the leather industry has been largely removed shoemaking continues, by far the most conspicuous occupation. Today it is mainly for the domestic market. Plastic, rexine and rubber are the raw materials, although never quite as raw as the youthful labour which is also used up on their manufacture. Working conditions are oppressive and stifling. Narrow pathways between huts and houses – many less than a metre wide – divide rooms without ventilation or natural light, in which eight or ten men and boys are making chappals. These vary in style from functional rubber footwear to the most delicate slippers embroidered with sequins, beads and gold or silver thread. Much of the production is now inferior throwaway items – insubstantial sandals and casual footwear for local use, providing some protection against stones and glass that litter the footpaths between buildings.

Most units are narrow box-like chambers, the roof scorched by the sun and scoured by hot humid winds: some structures are divided into three tiers, one half-below street level, one above, and a third reached by a ladder; while the fan, rotating like a great metal insect, only stirs the feverish air. The floors are covered with plastic, and discarded strips of material that remain when the shape of soles has been cut, abandoned on the ground, like footprints instructing some mad dance-steps.

I was more moved by this sight than I could have imagined, since my own family had been leatherworkers, and my uncles boasted that they could cut out soles from a skin, leaving virtually no waste. Although these young men were working on low-quality plastic, the skill was identical to that I had been expected to admire as a child. I had not been particularly impressed then; but to watch the careful paring of material here brought back a poignant memory; and, above all, the sameness of people in all cultures, races, faiths and social relationships in their sometimes heroic efforts to survive.

The men sat cross-legged, gluing shiny cross-straps, attaching soles to uppers, paring and pressing; a touching spectacle in the unwinking watchfulness of white strip-lighting that hummed in the silence, the front of each unit open to the parched breeze that entered through snaking stony pathways deepened by running waste water. Each unit, open to the street, was a theatrical tableau depicting unceasing labour. Some young men are bare-chested, others wear a banyan that is a lattice of holes. They wear either a lungi or shorts. The smell of glue is a pervasive reminder of its addictive property, and the smoke from cooking fires in the alley is trapped and spreads in furls of ghostly blue – a materialisation of the evaporating youth and beauty of the young men, the dark tangle of hair beneath their arms and the glistening sheen of the chest, the white sliver of a smile piercing the tainted air. They work a ten- or twelve-hour day, hours which also work on them in ways that the 150–200 rupees ($3–4) can scarcely compensate. In every unit there are young boys – some as young as nine or ten – ostensibly 'learning' for a daily reward of 50 rupees ($1).

There must be hundreds of such units in Tiljala Road and the adjacent neighbourhoods. I was drawn to them by memory of my own family, and found much heartbreakingly familiar. Mohammad Shakir was sitting in the lower part of a brick building divided horizontally into three storeys to create more workspace. He is 19. He has been working in various factories for four years, making two-dozen pairs of chappals a day and earning 200 rupees. His father, who migrated from the Sunderbans, does the same work. Mohammad Shakir is one of four children. It is his ambition to become an employer. Each pair of the high-class chappals he makes costs 130 rupees (about $3) in the market. With four men employed in the unit, he calculates that when raw materials have been bought, and rent and electricity paid, the owner must make between 10 and 20 rupees profit per pair. With four workers, that means almost 2000 rupees profit per day. Nothing is wasted in the unit. The scrap material stands ready in jute bags, awaiting collection in the alley outside the factory. Mohammad Shakir sleeps in the workshop, although it is without natural light and air. The house where his family lives is too small for him: he also serves as a kind of unofficial guard for the property, and gains nocturnal privacy. The employment is, in any case, not regular. At time of *puja* festivals and Eid orders are plentiful, but at other times of year there may be little or no work. Employees have no loyalty to the owners and roam from place to place in search of work, slightly higher pay, shorter hours or more regular labour. As we are talking, another worker returns to the unit. He is Mohammad Taslim, a middle aged man with a greying beard. He says, 'What hope is there for the poor? Politicians promise but do not perform.' He has two children, one aged ten and the other three. Of course he does not want them to work in such a place, but 'Fortune will decide what our children do. It is too early to know. It is written. It is their *kismat*.'

## VIII
## THE CHILD-BRIDE

The shoe industry is predominantly male, although some girls work at home where male eyes will not see the gentle curve of their neck, lowered eyes and buffalo-black braids of hair, in the brief interval between their flowering and their destiny as brides.

Razia Begum, a slender young woman of 30, was married in 1992 when she was 13. It is the aim of many parents to get their girls married as soon as possible because, in a world of predatory and unfulfilled male desire – tangible as the smoky air of the densely packed hutments – marriage is regarded as the most secure place for a girl. Razia Begum has been a victim of this cruel but persistent illusion. She has maintained her sensitive face and delicate frame; it is as though something had frozen her in an adolescence that proved so painful.

Her mother had to declare her daughter was 18 years old for the marriage to take place. Although child marriage is illegal, it is not difficult to circumvent laws which are applied flexibly, casually or not at all. Razia's parents provided her with a dowry of 3000 rupees in cash, as well as furniture, a watch, clothes, and household goods and utensils for her husband's family. The husband was a mechanic, and it seemed their daughter would be safe within her marital family. But after marriage, the husband simply stopped working. Within a short time, it became clear that Razia Begum's parents had made a sad mistake in their haste to see her settled and provided for. When the relationship was irretrievably broken, Razia Begum's in-laws refused her food and sustenance, and ordered her to leave their home. It was not that they were poor – her father-in-law worked for Kolkata Corporation – but they said they would not support her until her husband found work. To make him do so was a task beyond her; so, at 14, with a baby of three months, she was forced into the public shame of returning to her parental home.

With the help of a women's organisation, a legal case was brought against her husband and his family, on the grounds that he had failed to maintain her. He was held for a time in prison, but released on bail. He expressed his remorse to Razia Begum and promised everything would change. He would take care of her. He swore he had learned his lesson and things would be different. She relented and returned to him. 'For four or five months he was kind to me. He worked and earned money. Then one day he asked me to withdraw all legal cases against him.' She was advised by friends not to do so, but the pressure to believe in her husband was so great that she did as he wanted. Then she was trapped. After a few weeks, he became as he had been before. He then left her, and she has heard nothing of him since.

That was about 15 years ago. Since his desertion, she has brought up her son alone, with the help of her own parents. Razia Begum works in three houses as a maidservant, earning 200 rupees per month in each ($4). She also buys damaged fruit from the wholesale fruit market – bananas, oranges and apples – and sells them in the street. From this she earns 50–100 rupees daily ($1–2). She works as a cleaner in the local school, and opens it up in the morning. This provides her with another 200 rupees per month. She has struggled to keep her boy – now 16 – at school. Razia Begum would like him to become a doctor, but does not realise that with her limited resources this will remain what she says it is – a dream.

There are many such women in Tiljala, divorced or deserted, but few have the determination of Razia Begum. Her husband sold her marriage jewellery before he disappeared. Male vagabondage is often regarded as inevitable; and if a wife cannot hold her husband, it is she who will be considered at fault, even though in this case Razia Begum was herself only a child at the time of her marriage. Childhood itself is, in any case, a fragile construct in these places because children must work, take on the responsibility of younger siblings and sometimes marry before they are of an age to give informed consent. Legal definitions of childhood falter against custom and social necessity, just as campaigns to 'eliminate child labour' fall apart in the presence of families without food or livelihood.

I asked Razia Begum how it had come about that her parents married her so early. She said her mother-in-law had come from outside into the neighbourhood, and her parents invited her to their home. Her family are hard-working, honest and innocent; her father is a fish-seller. The negotiations were conducted very quickly. Her parents subsequently regretted their haste, and have done all they can to help their daughter. Razia Begum is one of three girls, which also explains the desire to see her married swiftly. Her youngest sister is still unmarried, because the prospective groom's family demand 50,000 rupees (over $1000). It has also been impossible for Razia to marry again, 'for who will marry a woman with children?'

I met Razia Begum again two or three months later and visited her house, a low-built but neatly-kept two-room hut. Her mother was selling fruit in the lane outside. Ten people live here – Razia Begum's third sister, her husband and three children, and Sultana, her youngest sister, a smiling young woman of 22 who was preparing the midday meal. It is now time for Sultana to be married, but where will the money come from for the dowry, which will cost a great deal more than was paid at the time of her sister's marriage. Dowry-inflation, it seems, is even higher than that of basic necessities. I said to her that the bride's beauty ought to be dowry enough. She blushed and said, 'Who will think of it in that way?'

Women are vulnerable, and at the same time strong: socially at risk by behaving independently or doing anything to incur suspicion that they have injured family 'honour'; yet when they are alone, widowed or abandoned, they show tenacity and resilience in bringing up their children, in defying convention, in the ingenuity they show in economic survival.

That men are powerful appears in poor communities as little more than a conventional fiction, maintained by women to keep from men the truth that their strength is fraudulent, at best bullying and bluster. The real reason why women must be guarded by a male relative is that unless they submit to this necessity, they may reveal themselves as the true agents of social stability, those who endure everything which society or fate (those inseparable twins) reserves for them. Men may use their privilege to neglect their children, to squander their money on drink, drugs or gambling; they may refuse to work and turn away from duty; they may run away, behave like spoiled children themselves, boast and even display their 'power' by beating women. If they do so, it is because they know that it is slipping from their tightening grasp. Such an apprehension, however dim, leads naturally to a greater assertiveness, to a louder declaration of their superiority. Women are not fooled; but they indulge their men, to save them from confronting what they know – that they are resourceless in the presence of need, and it is the women by whose tenacity and generosity they survive. Just as the poor are indispensable to the rich, who despise and stigmatise them, so it is with men and their status of fragile authority.

## IX
## THE VILLAGE IN THE CITY

Tiljala Road is really a collection of communities, and although two-thirds of its inhabitants were born here, many retain family connections with their villages of origin. Some people also pursue older cultural traditions, ancient rural practices: in the absence of the money to provide health care in the city, people often maintain folk-medicine based on roots, plants, herbs and tree-bark, familiar remedies still available in the city market-places. Here, too, the dying music of traditional culture may be heard, faint now, drowned out by the noisy clamour of commerce.

Beside the railway line, almost opposite Park Circus station, stands Darapada, the village of drums, where families still earn a livelihood from making toys, small miracles of inventiveness, a mixture of old craft and modern materials. Empty tins of adhesive paint are stacked outside the huts. These are cut down and the gut of slaughtered animals stretched across top and bottom, tied with thread to create a bright-coloured *dara* or drum; the treated intestines form a taut skin at top and bottom of the vessel. As well as drums, little carts are also made with a base of clay; clay wheels attached to drumsticks which play on the material drawn tightly over the shallow clay vessel, as the little cart is pulled along by a string. The faster the cart is drawn, the quicker the drumroll. The families sell the toys in local fairs and markets. Mohammad Ginger lives here with his eight family members. Their hut is packed with tins and the treated gut, which nevertheless retains a faint smell of decayed animal matter. Mohammad Ginger says their grandfathers came here 60 or 70 years ago. Their land had been lost, and for a time they had been *borga* workers or sharecroppers. Their village is Basirhat, close to the border with Bangladesh, a place which had preserved some of these ancient self-reliant folk-arts. It is a sad paradox, that poverty is the most effective preserver of traditional cultures. Unchanging societies require not change, but continuity; a tension that lies at the heart of debate among Muslims about an education suitable for conservative values in a world in which everything is in a state of rapid and convulsive transformation.

The earnings from the craft of toymaking are modest – Mohammad Ginger makes between 3,000 and 4,000 rupees per month. One of his boys is working full-time and the other children help with toy-making in their leisure time from school. He shows his proudest accomplishment – the small one-string violin, the *ektara*, which is played to accompany traditional songs. He sings a few bars of an old folk-tune:

*Bondhu tin din tor barite gelam*
*Dekha pailam na.*

For three days, friend, I waited by your house, but you never came.

They live and sleep in the hut amid the collection of tins, the smell of paint and a residual scent of animals. The room is high and airless. In the small kitchen in front of the workshop/living area, Mohammad Ginger's wife is making lunch; a masala omelette in a blackened pan. It is a precarious life, since the ingenuity of the old folk arts is now being rapidly undermined by plastic toys and inert but showy objects from China. Just as they were removed from their land two or three generations ago, now they are being evicted from a craft which sustained them during the move to the city. It is a touching sight - the little drums that sell at 10–15 rupees and the ektara for 8–10 rupees. When there are no local or village fairs, they go door-to-door in Tiljala Road and the adjacent areas, but their poor people's wisdom, with its ability to re-cycle and save discarded goods, is itself an archaic skill, doomed to slow extinction in a wasting world.

Bahar Ali also used to make *dharas* and other toys, but he is now in his 60s; stringy, wearing a lungi and big glasses that magnify his eyes. His family migrated to Kolkata when they lost their land during his childhood in the Sunderbans. The old skills have died in his hands, which have grown clumsy and aged, and he has no one to whom he can transmit them – the true burden of being old, old and guilty, since who can see old crafts wither without a pang of regret and self-blame? His wife, Mumtaz, received microcredit from Tiljala-SHED to work as a fruitseller. When she talks of their life, it is a terrible song of loss. Four girls died in infancy – aged two, one, three years, and a few months old. Death, she says, has been the most frequent guest in their poor house. Her 15-year-old son died of kidney failure. If people complain that Muslims have large families, Mumtaz Begum will take them to the cemetery and show them where her five children lie. There are three married sons: one works repairing air-conditioning and refrigeration, another drives an autorickshaw, while the third is a daily labourer on construction sites. They have modernised their skills and adapted to urban life in ways that will assure them of a reasonable livelihood; which their parents were unable to do. 'A new generation requires new talents', says Mumtaz. 'But old people are at the mercy of their children. Life was a challenge when we were young, and it remains so.' To eat well, Mumtaz claims that her family of nine people require at least 200 rupees daily, which is beyond their means. They pay a low monthly rent of 50 rupees, and 300 rupees for their light and fan. Life is constrained: two sons, one with a wife and child, the other with his wife and two children, share a space so small that, unless they all breathe together, someone will be blown out of the house.

Mumtaz laments,

> We have lost the old relationships with sisters and brothers. We lost them and do not know where they are. In the crush of poverty, everything is forgotten, even loved ones. Relationships fall apart and families separate, go their own ways. If I ask my relatives even for a plate of rice, they will say, 'Oh today I cooked less than usual, how can I give?'

Bahar Ali and his wife have a Below Poverty Line card, which entitles them to subsidised foodstuffs and household necessities, but they say it is worthless. The five kilos of rice to which they are entitled a week is scarcely edible, adulterated with stones. They get one bar of soap and a box of matches a week. Life here is tense and uncomfortable. 'There is always fighting between the gangs of the various politicians. Nobody disturbs us because we are old, and everybody knows we have nothing, so why would they bother with us?'

## X
## THE WIDOW'S TALE

Algoni Begum is a member of a widows' project run by Tiljala-SHED. Her husband died in 1999. She sells rice, and makes a daily profit of 50–70 rupees. She lives with her son, and his wife and family. Her son was recently injured in a 'war' between gangs battling for control of part of Tiljala. 'He was a member of one gang, and was injured when a bomb was thrown. One side of his body was paralysed and he could not work for many months. Now he has a small tea shop. During the time he was sick, we passed difficult days.' What causes the fights? The old woman is vague. 'They fight to control the land between different interests.' Those who 'own' the neighbourhood give protection to the small traders and businesses for payment of a regular sum. Algoni Begum's family came from South 24 Parganas, but that was a long time ago. She was born here. She also spoke of a recent practice, which we were to hear from several women. She now buys ready-cooked food from dhabas and small restaurants, since it is becoming too expensive to buy rice, vegetables and dal for preparation at home. 'We buy *nan-roti* from outside with some vegetable. It is cheaper than buying expensive ingredients, especially since the price of cooking fuel and oil has also risen.' Mumtaz Begum said she is doing the same thing; perhaps only as a temporary expedient while prices are so high. Or perhaps not. If it becomes a regular feature of the lives of the poor, this will lead to a lowering of their nutritional status. It also involves de-skilling, so that the ability of poor people to provide the greatest possible nutrition with very little money is undermined. It is difficult to know whether this is a distinct social trend, or a few isolated examples of people led by poverty to new extremes.

## XI
## MEDICAL CARE

Outside a small brick building, a sign of a green cross on a white background announces one of many private doctors' surgeries in Tiljala Road. It is, like all the buildings, inadequate for its purpose, and although there are only a few patients inside, it feels overcrowded. On a concrete ledge, sits a young boy of about 14. His right leg has been badly burned. The flesh is red and raw from the knee to the ankle, an ugly suppurating wound, which is being dressed by a young man, an aide to the doctor. The patient is Shahbuddin. He was recently in the procession at the time of the festival of Muharram. Someone had taught him how to breathe fire. You take a mouthful of petrol, ignite it on the tongue and then blow hard, so that a great jet of flame appears to come out of your mouth. In the excitement, some lighted petrol fell on to his jeans, and at first he did not notice it, since he was so carried away with his own prowess. By the time he became aware of the pain, the burn to his leg had become severe. The young man dressing the wound covers the exposed flesh with a layer of betadine, gently places a layer of gauze and then applies silverex antibiotic ointment.

Shahbuddin is now recovering. He smiles wanly. His mother, Asma, and grandmother, Sabra, are with him. 'A week ago he was crying with pain and could not move.' His mother works as a maidservant, and earns 1100 rupees per month. Her husband is dead. He fell sick with a fever. They did not realise how serious it was, and by the time they reached hospital with him, it was too late. Shahbuddin is learning tailoring, for which he is paid 250 rupees per week. This sum is essential for the family's needs, so his mother is anxious he should return to his duties as soon as possible. He is the only boy. His mother has brought one of her girls to see the doctor, suffering from a cough and chest infection.

The surgery is a spare, austere place with the walls painted green. There is a glass-fronted cupboard containing basic drugs, a wooden desk and some stools. The women say that the doctor is trustworthy and helpful to the poor. His charges are very low and if the people have nothing, he treats them without payment. Sabra says that if they had taken Shahbuddin to hospital, he would almost certainly have lost his leg.

The doctor, a modest young man, wears a white coat and a stethoscope around his neck, as he is expected to do. He has a Diploma in Indo–Allopathic Medicine, which he gained through the distance learning university. It takes two years after graduation before the diploma is given. He comes from Midnapur, but is living nearby. He and his colleagues are fighting for full recognition from the government, which has – in the face of opposition from the medical profession – recently announced it will use alternative or 'barefoot' doctors to help extend health care coverage to remote villages and poor urban areas, many of which are at the mercy of barely qualified and unscrupulous practitioners. The doctor has been in Tiljala Road for five years, and has earned his reputation for being considerate to poor people. He says proudly. 'We have made progress. The government formerly did not accept a death certificate from us; but now they do.' Whether one should regard this as an improvement, or as yet more evidence that the death of the poor is of as small account to authority as their life, it is difficult to know.

## XII
## THE IMAM

We met Mohammad Ibrahim, imam of the largest mosque in Tiljala. This is a well-constructed stone building with coloured glass windows and an imposing entrance – a very different institution from the more humble mosque of Topsia. Mohammad Ibrahim wears a cream-coloured kamiz and a white lace topi. He has a carefully trimmed grey beard. He greets us warmly. He acknowledges the obvious – that poor people come less to the *masjid* and observe religious duties less zealously than the better off. 'Illiteracy is easily exploited. People have to work, and *pardah* cannot be maintained. Sometimes, political parties come, but they only cause trouble. Muslims are brothers, and should not be separated by divisive politics that have nothing to do with religion.' He says, 'We have been increasing the number of our worshippers, since we sent out a group of preachers into the neighbourhood.

They tell the people, 'This world is a guest house. You live in paradise, and tomorrow, or even today, you could be there.' This has had some effect.

While we were talking a young boy caught my eye and smiled. He was smartly dressed in school uniform, and he listened intently to everything that was said. He then followed us through the streets for the next half hour. His name was Rahmat. He was studying, but finding it very difficult, because his father had left the family, and he must work to help feed his brother and continue his studies. He was looking for a sponsor. He took my hand, both trusting and proprietorial. When we came to the railway line and had to part, he would not let go. Tearfully, he left us, but turned round two or three times as if in supplication, until we were lost to sight.

## XIII
## THE LIFE OF THE DEAD

Perhaps because death has been a familiar companion in the slums, many people express fear of spirits and ghosts. They are truly haunted by the memory of babies who died in the night without apparent cause, or of the child who chose to leave life, as one woman said, because he could not bear the suffering of the people. There are three Muslim graveyards on the edge of Tiljala Road which, on a fine Thursday morning, were crowded with people. These are places where life and death meet, and the two are separated only by the thinnest membrane. You can walk so easily from one to the other; and it is a two-way traffic, as the ubiquitous djinns and spirits testify. The archway announcing the place of the dead leads into a great tranquil compound, shaded by soaring trees, raintrees, ashokas, mangoes and fish-tail palms, no doubt fertilised by the human remains which promote their luxuriant growth, with the result that the cemetery has the air of a botanical garden rather than a necropolis.

There is a tank, a pond with steps leading down into deep glaucous water, where men and children are bathing; mature men in lungis, the children naked and sleek; a place not so much for ritual cleansing as for an exuberant re-affirmation of life in this solemn place. Two burials are taking place simultaneously. The open coffin is borne aloft by six men, while others follow, many in Islamic dress, some consoling the bereaved. A yellow cloth covers the body, which is dressed in a white cerement, but the face is uncovered as the dead man is lowered into the open grave.

Many graves are covered with a flimsy *chador* – a red or yellow length of muslin with a gold border, dingy with dust and rain, covering the mound and held in place by stones. This, explains Imran, is a gesture of dignity, not because the dead are cold, but a mark of respect, to cover the nakedness of the earth to which they are exposed.

We sat on the verandah of the burial office. Why are women not allowed in graveyards? It is, someone says, because the souls of the recently dead hover close to the surface and some evil spirit may enter their body. No, says another, it is because of the menstrual cycle of women. Burial has to take place on the day of the death, because within hours of death angels interrogate the deceased as to how far he or she has observed the tenets of the faith, and fulfilled the obligations demanded by Islam.

Sheikh Munna is a gravedigger. Bare-chested, he wears a lungi and a *tabiz* on his upper right arm. He is a physically powerful young man of 26. His father, grandfather and great-grandfather did this work before him, and his son will continue in his turn. He lives in a house in the graveyard, and is paid 3000 rupees a month by the Kolkata Corporation, as well as whatever gratuity the families of the dead choose to give him.

In the graveyard, we met an elderly man who, by chance, is attending the funeral of a relative. He stopped us and asked me if I thought justice had been done to his nephew. This man is the uncle of Rizwan ur Rahman, whose death two years ago caused a great scandal in the city, and still reverberates angrily in popular memory. Rizwan was a graphic designer, an educated young Muslim, who had fallen in love with and married Priyanka Todi, the daughter of a rich Hindu family of industrialists. They had studied together and made a love-marriage. The Todi family had done its best to separate them. The young man later disappeared. Some time later, his body was found close to the railway line in Tiljala. The police declared it a case of suicide even before the post mortem had taken place, although it was widely believed to have been murder. His house was close to the railway line, but he had gone a kilometre or more before stepping in front of the train. Nothing was proved, and despite an investigation by the Central Bureau of Investigation, no evidence was produced to link the influential Hindu family to the death of their son-in-law. Failure to pursue this case with due rigour became a *cause celebre*, evidence to many Muslims that there is a conspiracy against them, even those who become successful on the terms of a society, which does not want to acknowledge either their contribution or even their presence. This rejection lies at the root of a growing communal apartheid; of which these slums, far from being an archaic relic, are also forerunners and anticipatory warnings of things to come.

The Rizwan case remains unresolved. The death of this young Muslim is believed by many people in Tiljala to have been covered up by the ruling party, which likes to proclaim its secular credentials. The case was taken up by the Opposition Trinamool Congress Party, and the brother of Rizwan was a candidate in the municipal elections in 2010. There is nothing that cannot be politicised. Rizwan's uncle says, 'The Opposition descends like vultures wherever there are victims. Rizwan's family are being exploited and used as for propaganda, to show the nexus between police and the CPI(M)'.

In the event, Rizwan's brother lost the election to the candidate of a party supporting the Communist Party of India. Many people in the area felt it had been an opportunistic candidacy. Rizwan's uncle also stood for election, against his nephew; stories were circulating that he had done so in order to undermine the vote for his relative. Intrigue and counter-intrigue mark the electoral practices not only of the CPI(M) but also of the Trinamool Congress, from whose dominance of the politics of Kolkata, from May 2010, little positive outcome is expected, particularly for the poor people of Kolkata.

## XIV
## THE GRAVEYARD BEGGARS

We came across Amina Bibi, an old arthritic woman with a seamed face and without teeth. She was sitting on a length of polythene at the root of a palm-tree in a secluded part of the burial-ground. She wore a faded green saree, plastic chappals and a grubby blouse. Amina Bibi has severe pain in her back and cannot move, except by shuffling slowly. She used to beg near the cemetery gate which has been closed, so that she is now unable to reach the place where food and alms are distributed. She says no one comes this side any more, only the spirits whispering in the trees. She is lucky to earn 15–20 rupees per day (about $0.50). Her daughter is physically handicapped. Her son drinks chulai, but he, too, had an accident when he was drunk. The whole family lives by begging, including her little granddaughter Yasmin Khatoon, a child of about nine, barefoot and wearing nothing but a pair of dark pants.

At the main gate of the cemetery sit the elderly and the infirm, waiting for food, begging money of mourners passing in and out, for it is known that the newly bereaved generally have tender hearts. A woman of about 40, Zarina, is sitting in a big black wheelchair. She cannot speak, but smiles and gesticulates in greeting. Her aunt, Hayatur, is with her, an elderly woman, perhaps in her late 60s. Together, they make between 15 and 20 rupees a day. Zarina has always been without speech, but until her legs were injured in a train accident, she used to clean vegetables in people's houses. That they manage to survive by begging says much about the never exhausted charity of the poor.


## XV
## THE GOVERNMENT SCHOOL

We visited a government school, Panka Jini, close to the burial-ground. It faces the main road, but has limited space, with desks too close together and little light. The teachers sit at a metal desk: a portrait of Subhash Chandra Bose, a calendar and a blackboard are the only objects in a room which looks as though it were designed for an experiment in sensory deprivation. The school, a pre-primary, was established in 1973, for children living in the social penumbra, between cemetery and railway line.

Many of the children are very small, but they have a knowingness that has turned them into miniature adults – like the iconography of childhood in Western Renaissance painting. Zeenat Tarafdar's father collects scrap iron. He lives beside the railway line, but has never been in a train. He does not like living here. He is afraid of the noise and the violence. He remembers the night of the communal fight between Muslims and Hindus in October 2009, which was centred around the huts along the tracks. At night, he says, the police threw tear-gas shells, and the smoke hurt his throat and eyes. He is ten years old, but fears tension and fighting between the communities. A sensitive child, he also does not like to see the men drinking *daru* or playing cards, because then they beat each other. He would like to be a doctor – perhaps the most frequently articulated ambition of poor children in the slums. This should not be necessarily taken at face value, for it indicates, not so much a possible career path, as the fact that even small children recognise that the greatest need of the world into which they have been born is for healing.

Sultana Parveen lives with her mother in a hut along the tracks. They have lived alone since her father died. She is a grave child, forthright and with a clear understanding of social relationships between rich and poor. When she was very small, her father died of heart disease. Although she was four at the time, she knew it was because they were too poor to buy medicine. Sultana is now nine. Her mother is a servant in seven separate houses. Most days she manages to bring home some leftover food. She leaves their hut at four o'clock in the morning, the address of which is Number 1, Cemetery Railway Lines. Sultana gets up at seven, washes her teeth and buys *chanachur* snacks before going to school. Between four and seven in the morning, she remains alone. She then goes to where her mother is working and hands her the key. If there is any food at her mother's workplace, she will eat before going to school. Her mother returns about three o'clock in the afternoon. Sultana has lunch and then goes to a lady teacher for tuition. Mother then goes back to work until six o'clock. She prepares food, after which they sleep. Mother sometimes asks Sultana to massage the pains in her neck and back. When she speaks, the child tells of a bare, austere existence, not a life, only a sketch of living.

Sultana says there is always a battle for water, since the tap is in the authorised settlement, and they resent people from the railway colony going there. She does not like to see people openly drinking liquor, and she is afraid of them when they are drunk. Although she is peaceful, her mother is often disturbed by people who are noisy and quarrelsome. Her mother objects, and this makes the drinkers angry. If there is enough leftover food, Sultana's mother also distributes it to other needy people nearby.

The teachers are sympathetic, and show tenderness and affection to the children. If they feel a sense of helplessness, this is partly because they learn as much from their pupils as the children do from them. 'At least', says the headmaster, 'the school provides some scope for poor children. They are much more intelligent than they are given credit for, but the opportunities for that intelligence to flower do not exist. Many of the children go with their mother to help out as tiny maidservants, and at home, they have their own duties. The fathers are often absent or drinking. Although most men work conscientiously, some have no sense of responsibility. They marry someone else; and when they tire of the new one, they come back.'

## XVI
## THE LITTLE GIRLS

After school, the little girls wanted to take us to their home along the railway tracks. Their trust was poignant, as they skipped along, holding our hand. What an incongruous little procession we made, three or four small girls, three adult men, one a foreigner. Such a sight would never present itself in Britain; and although there are, doubtless, predators in these neighbourhoods as elsewhere, there is little suspicion that strangers lie in wait to damage children. There are other, more prominent agents of abuse and hurt – hunger, want and a maturity thrust upon them by poverty, the neediness of parents.

We walked back through the cemetery. I asked Sultana if she knew what the cemetery is for. How could she not know? She said 'The people here are only shadows. They live in another world. You cannot see them, but you know they are there.' And then, as if to reassure me, she said with her child's wisdom 'They will do us no harm.'

We came out onto the railway track. The grey granite chips hurt the feet even through the soles of shoes. We reached Sultana's hut. It is about a metre high, covered with polythene, with bamboo frame and walls. Shaded by a tree, the crinkled yellow bell of a creeper had also made its way across the roof, pushing out its pale tendrils among the dust that has collected in the folds of black material. Sultana's mother has not yet returned. Sarina, another child who has accompanied us, urges us to visit her house. Her father, Mohammad Bahul, is sitting outside with some neighbours. His leg is in plaster. He was injured in the riot of October 2009, which was clearly more serious than had been reported at the time. For three months he has been unable to work as an electrician because he cannot walk. His family came long ago from Bihar. His wife is a maidservant. He has three daughters and one son; one daughter lives with her grandmother. The rough shelters are made of *chetai*, wood and industrial sacking. He says the mafia built the huts and sub-let them to the people. It was worth 10,000 rupees, but if he were to sell it now, he could do so for 20,000 rupees (about $450), despite the fact that this is not a legal structure. But no one is going to demolish it, because the owners and the government are close, and in any case, it was their people who built it.

## XVII
## 'DEVELOPING' THE SLUMS

Leaving the graveyard, we went back into the Tiljala Road settlement. In a small workshop open to the street – more cell than shop – two boys were doing embroidery work for slippers. Tough red or white material is stretched tightly over an embroidery frame, and the two young men stitch beads and spangles according to a design embossed on the fabric; each tiny gold bead and crystal lies in a velvet tray, and is picked up by the needle and threaded meticulously into the tissue. The square of material has space for perhaps a dozen individual pieces of decorative work, which will be cut and attached to the sole of the shoe. The young men are paid 200 rupees a day ($4.40). It is exhausting, close work, and the strip lighting throws a shadowless glare over where they sit cross-legged on a length of plastic cloth on the concrete. Each pair of these superior slippers will be sold to a middleman for 300 rupees, but many will go for export to Singapore or America where a pair will sell for 3000 rupees ($65). From Howrah, Javed has been working here for four years; his companion Raju came from Bihar only six months ago. They live in the unit: their drinking water bottles beside them, and a change of clothing hanging from a nail in the wall; stark, exiguous lives of people working a ten- or twelve-hour day, producing objects of great beauty and artistry, for which their remuneration remains pitiful. Each boy sends home 2000 rupees a month.

As we walked between two new buildings, four or five-storeys high, we were approached by an elderly woman with short curly hair, wearing a navy-blue dress. She heard us talking about the construction of the brick buildings which are replacing the small one-room structures, many of which have stood here for 50 or 60 years. The woman introduced herself with old-fashioned courtliness as 'Mrs Mitchell.' She was, she said, Anglo–Indian, of whom many lived in the neighbourhood until about 20 years ago. She invited us into her ground-floor room in a new building. It was scoured and swept clean, and above the bed there was an image of Christ on the cross, with, below him, a small altar with a length of sky-blue material around it.

Mrs Mitchell was born in 1942. Her father worked in the Indian railways. He had a brother, also a railwayman and a sister who was a nurse. Mrs Mitchell still has relatives in

Streatham, south London. She was taken there as a child, but can scarcely remember it. She has preserved in memory an idealised London, a place of civility, politeness and cleanliness. She occasionally calls her relatives by telephone, but they do not return her calls. She contrasts the London of her imagination with the all-too-real Kolkata of daily experience.

She was particularly vulnerable at the moment when we met her. Her husband had died a month earlier. He had contracted brain malaria and was admitted to hospital the same day, but within hours he was dead.

She sits on her bed, which is covered with a brown and silver throw. From beneath the pillow she takes out a pair of blue and white shorts that belonged to her husband. 'I keep these to remember him by.' She touches her cheek tenderly with the material and weeps a few tears. 'I'm a Christian, of course. I go to St James' Church which is nearby, nearly opposite Mother Teresa's tomb. He was twelve years older than I am. 79. I miss him so much.'

She was formerly employed as a housekeeper at the Radisson Hotel, but she says there were too many trade union problems that she could not cope with, so she left. Although she is 67, she still has to earn a livelihood, which she does by giving English tuition. 'Fortunately, I have that gift of good English, otherwise I do not know how I would earn enough to keep myself.' This legacy of her British connection at least allows her to survive.

Mrs Mitchell's experience demonstrates what is happening with the new construction in Tiljala Road. The landlord – the theka tenant – sold her small house along with those of some neighbours. He re-housed her and her husband temporarily while the new building was being erected. They were then given a room at the same rent – only 56 rupees per month – in accordance with the law.

> But it is smaller than the space we had before. And then even before my husband was buried, the rent was raised. After his death, the landlord changed the name on the bill to mine, and as soon as that happens, they are allowed to raise the rent. He also demanded 30,000 rupees. Where will I ever find so much money?
>
> The promoter built the house, and while construction was taking place, he paid our rent for six months in a small house close by. All the promoter has to do is get the landlord's signature, and although the tenants are also supposed to affirm that they have no objection, this is seen as a formality. Our original room was 12 feet by 12; this is 10 by 10, so they have already chopped off enough from the original floorspace to create an extra room on the ground floor. The rooms above the ground floor are sold for two or three lakh of rupees ($2500), *salami* style, which the new occupants pay to the builder, a fixed amount per square foot. I pay rent to the theka tenant who has made the business with the builder, but that amount is controlled by law. Only the new owners on the upper floors pay the full rent, or buy the room. The contractor gets his profit and the building reverts to the theka tenant when they have agreed on a share-out of the profit. The present building is illegal. The promoter had permission to build ground floor plus two storeys – in fact he has built four.

These buildings are close together, hastily erected without regard to the existing infrastructure. The sheer numbers who live in them are both the greatest guarantee of security to the people (governments would hesitate to demolish), but this is, paradoxically, at the same time a source of great potential instability – the risk of collapse is always there. When the value of land rises to a certain level, there is no doubt they will be swept away. Mrs Mitchell feels exposed: alone, widowed, her room is worth a considerable sum to the landlord. She says she will not be intimidated. In any case, God will protect her.

I visited Mrs Mitchell again a few months later. The landlord stopped taking the rent, and would not transfer the tenancy to Mrs Mitchell without payment of the large sum he had demanded. The aim of the landlord in refusing the rent is to make it appear that the tenants are defaulting, so he can get a court order to evict them. Mrs Mitchell is paying the rent to the office of the Rent Controller, so that the landlord will not be able to declare that she has failed to maintain payment. He is still insisting on 30,000 rupees to change the name on the tenancy agreement to hers.

Since her husband died, a little Hindu girl from the place where they were temporarily housed comes every night to keep her company and sleep with her. She goes to school in the day and comes to share Mrs Mitchell's meal at night because her family are also poor. 'They call me Auntie.' It is a great comfort to her to feel the child's warmth at night. She is twelve.

But I remember him all the time. When I first married him, I didn't like him much. He was my brother's friend. When I was young, I wanted to be a nun, I didn't want to marry at all. But I was forced to. At first, I resented it, and didn't like him. But with time, I came to love him. He never set a hand on me. We had 45 years together. He was a jewel of a husband. He made his peace with God before he died. He said to me 'Ma, I love you.' He called me into the ward, and said, 'Don't go.' He was very ill. I said, 'Jesus, bring him back, even in the same state he is now, I'll look after him.' I still fall asleep crying. And I go to the cemetery to sit beside him.

One morning, I was preparing some vegetables. Suddenly I felt a need to go to be with him. I left everything and went to Bhawanipur, where the Christian cemetery is. I sat there from ten o'clock in the morning till three in the afternoon. Then the *mali*, the gardener who looks after the graves, came and put his arm around me. He lifted me up and said, 'It's time to go now, mother. We're closing the gates.' It wasn't true. There was another funeral due at four o'clock. But he had seen that I had been there all day, and he knew it was not good for me. I was very touched that he had noticed and tried to help.'

She weeps old tears, moved by the stranger who had observed her grief and shown her one gesture of tender understanding.

## XVIII
## UNEMPLOYED YOUTH

In Tiljala, there are hundreds, if not thousands, of young unemployed men, men like Iqbal. An arrestingly handsome man, he has dark curly hair, compelling eyes and a luminous smile. At 25, he is married with two children. He is a member of a sports club founded by the ruling CPI(M). He left school when he was ten, and worked in leather units, roaming from one to another. All around him, he saw corruption, extortion, exploitation, illegal construction and people who got rich overnight. He now has more lucrative work, since he serves as a kind of unofficial policeman for the politicians. His youthful energy has found an outlet, in the name of political commitment to the welfare of the poor; he is part of the army of enforcers, who collect donations for the party, and protect the smugglers, thieves and 'anti-socials', who have become such significant agents in the party's retention of power. Here is a truly frightening phenomenon; the allegiance of such young men is certainly not to political ideals, but to whoever will pay them. Whether this is crime, political muscle-power or social destabilisation is a matter of indifference to them. Iqbal, and those like him, are mercenaries, who will fight, in theory on behalf on the poor and oppressed, the disfranchised of Tiljala, according to whatever ideology is in the ascendant. The relationship of these young men to the non-government organisations is one of benign neutrality – as long as they do not encroach upon their means of survival, they will co-exist. They constitute another minority, who also lead separate lives, lives of petty privilege and power; and it does not do to cross them. Since economic activity is the most obvious characteristic of these communities, the young men who do nothing are highly visible. Their indolence lets the people know who they are, since it says they are the hirelings of politicians, and therefore, protected by the rich and influential. This legitimates and sustains their apparent inactivity. In fact, they are the eyes and ears of absent masters.

## XIX
## THE LIBRARY

Tiljala-SHED has established a library in the community. This is scarcely calculated to disseminate dangerous ideas, since its books consist mainly of children's stories in Urdu and Bengali, and English-language text-books on accountancy, IT, law and business studies. There is little danger of stimulating the imagination or rousing – let alone raising – the consciousness of the people. The building does, however, serve as a meeting-point, and has rooms where children can be cared for while their mothers work, a night shelter for girls and a place for young women to meet and to play games – board games of Monopoly, Ludo, snakes and ladders. Legal aid and advice are available for deserted wives. A room with three computers enables young women to study IT. The building is staffed by Shama and Ismat, both 19, who are paid 3000 rupees, and whose educational expenses are borne by Associazione Italiana Donne per lo Sviluppo (AIDOS; Italian Association for Women in Development),[14] an Italian organisation which sponsors the education of poor girls.

Shama and Ismat are hopeful that they will complete their university studies and find work. They are both the first in their families to aspire to such heights. Shama's father is a tailor, Ismat's a car-washer. Shama has four sisters and one brother, Ismat five sisters. Shama is studying English and Political Science, Ismat, Urdu, Philosophy and History. Both families are originally from Bihar and, although Shama's family have a house there, Ismat has never been to Bihar. Rural belonging lingers, a faint yearning for the natural world, and perhaps also for conservative social values, exposed now to the disturbing influence of modernity. It has taken a great effort for the two girls, who are as eager, attentive and compliant in their studies as their sisters are in yielding to domestic duty and submission to the will of their husbands. Hope blooms, like the wild flowers that survive in the stony surface of a wall. They are simultaneously inspiring and vulnerable: for although Shama studies English, she finds it very difficult to understand and has never before met a native English speaker. It is a great misfortune that those who have no experience of education can be readily persuaded that what they are learning will transform their lives, even when what they are actually acquiring is elementary. It is as easy to exploit people in the name of education as it is in the interests of earning a livelihood.

## XX
## THE REWARDS OF LABOUR

Many houses in the Tiljala Road area now speak of a modest, hard-working sufficiency. Over the years, the old kacha buildings have been replaced by whitewashed brick walls and tiled roofs, and although it is impossible to extend the floor space to accommodate growing families, some have expanded upwards. The door of the house of Asghar Ali and Mumtaz Begum stands open, and you can see through the three rooms to the yard behind. A young man and a young woman are working at machines, stitching chappals. The man scarcely looks up from his work, but his co-worker, a daughter of the house, offers a dancing Bengali smile of welcome. She is stitching gold-coloured straps onto the back of chappals. The house shows signs of limited well-being: there is a glass-fronted cupboard which contains dusty china cups and a large wooden bedstead, but the floor is uncovered concrete. Asghar Ali is an electrician, and Mumtaz herself set up the workshop as the children were growing up. There are twin boys of 15, who both study and help with the work after school. One girl who was sponsored by AIDOS, is already married, and the other daughter, now 20, is to be married next month. A silent, self-effacing child of twelve, Mohammad Salim, is also present: he is collecting the finished soles to deliver them to the manufacturer who employs him. He earns 100 rupees per week (just over $2).

These children are everywhere in Tiljala, fetching and carrying, working in chappal factories, at tea-stalls, scouring the area for articles for re-cycling, welding cycle-rickshaw axles, cleaning and polishing, begging; so slight and unobtrusive they are scarcely visible; ghost-children, but whose slender income makes the difference to their families between a barely satisfactory diet and malnutrition.

Mumtaz Begum is paid between 6 and 20 rupees per dozen for the finished soles, according to the quality of the goods. I was intrigued by the story of the daughter whose education had been sponsored by AIDOS. Did she use her qualifications in any work-situation? That is not the point, I was told. Her education will help her become an enlightened wife and mother. Progress in the freedom of women cannot be carried forward so quickly. Let it suffice that she knows the value of education for both daughters and sons.

Asghar Ali has a series of stamping machines, with which he embosses the finished articles with the size of the chappal and the name of the manufacturer. The young man who does not interrupt his work is a partner in the business, and takes 50 per cent of the profit – about 200 rupees per day for each of them. Asghar Ali was born here, in this house. His grandfather had migrated to the area and built the house, at that time a temporary shelter, which he improved over time. If there are few luxuries, this is because of the inescapable demands of dowry. The daughter's wedding cost 50,000 rupees (Over $1000) just for the hire of the marriage hall and party. This is one way in which the poor stay poor; and because girls take with them a dowry, they are regarded by many as a liability. The children have to work after school as a contribution to their educational costs. Asghar Ali's brother is a businessman, and has become very rich. 'We never see him. The family is broken. Perhaps he doesn't want to meet us, because he is afraid we will ask him for money.'

Asghar Ali says the neighbourhood is not peaceful. There are often fights between different political factions and gangs.

If anyone disturbs me, I say to him 'You are my big brother' so that he can see that I submit to him. I know karate, and if I wanted to, I could fight and beat him, but I do not. When it comes to the marriage of my daughter, we have to be very careful, and find out who the groom is. We must be sure he is sincere and hard-working, free from addiction, a pious Muslim.

A majority of people in Tiljala Road are like Asghar Ali and Mumtaz Begum, although many struggle without achieving even the relative security of this family; a security always threatened by sickness, by unforeseen expense and by political violence. From time to time, fires sweep through the area – a kerosene lamp is overturned, a cooking fire runs out of control, but political arson is not unknown, in which whole areas are cleared for the benefit of promoters and developers. When I was in Kolkata in June 2009, a blaze gutted 80 shanties in Tiljala, leaving several hundred homeless. The fire was said to have started by residents using dried leaves and wood as cooking fuel. It spread so quickly because the structures are made of flammable material and many of them store goods that burn readily – soap, oil and waste paper.

People are unaware of the extent to which their lives are shaped by events beyond their control. Competition from cheap footwear from China can wipe out a whole industry. Laws against child labour enacted in Delhi can plunge a family back into poverty. Mistrust of Muslims in the United States, Europe or elsewhere in the rich world also hardens hearts in India and emboldens the majority to acts of gratuitous vengefulness. All this weighs upon the life of the people here, invisibly adding to already heavy burdens of poverty and prejudice. Alamgir tells how he was talking one day to a group of women about their rights and their children's rights,

> You know what they asked me? 'Alambhai, can you tell us in which market we can get these things?' You talk to people about the nutritional needs of pregnant women, pre-natal support, early childhood education. Very beautifully you explain and they ask, tell me where we can get it ... In which market ...

## XXI
## THE HOUSELESS MIND

An elderly man wanders Tiljala, collecting rubbish. He is deaf and dumb, and lives in the squatter settlement near the railway line. Although without speech, he has learned to communicate by gesture, a theatrical pantomime with expressive eyes and large hands. He has grey hair and beard, wears a vest reduced to lacy holes, a blue lungi, a steel bangle at his wrist and plastic chappals. He makes us understand that water is coming through the roof of his hut, so that he cannot sleep on the wet earthen floor. He wants someone to make a concrete base, so he can sweep and keep it clean. I ask his name. He indicates that he will write it down. On the margin of the *Times of India*, he writes an indecipherable scrawl, neither Urdu nor Bengali. No one knows who he is or where he came from. Probably close to 60, he has wandered the slum as long as anyone can remember. He does daily labour, carrying, loading and unloading 'vans'. He also cleans utensils in a local tea-shop, and together with the charity of neighbours, makes enough to feed and clothe himself.

His hut is made of metal and bamboo, and the roof is polythene. The door will scarcely open, since it is crammed from floor to ceiling with waste material – newspapers, tins, bottles, sacks, cardboard, boxes and plastic. The water does come through the roof, but it is difficult to see where he would sleep even if it were waterproof. In fact, he sleeps under the eaves of a neighbour's house, on a long concrete slab painted green; a bed that looks more like a funerary monument than a place of earthly rest.

Although he has been around so long he is part of the landscape, the idea of a man without antecedents, without village or family, is obscurely disturbing, since to be without these things is to be bereft of even the shreds of identity which people derive from family, kinsfolk or even a distant belonging to Bihar. That he is treated with compassion says much about the kindness of the poor people of Tiljala Road, who, despite their own poverty and disinheritance, do not allow the disabled, the weak, the slow-witted and the mentally unstable to go hungry.

## XXII
## A LOCAL DISTURBANCE

On the evening of 28 October 2009, there was a communal disturbance in the neighbourhood. It was the night of *Jagadhatri Puja*, one of the manifestations of Durga, whose idol was to be immersed in the river. This is one of the most benign incarnations of Durga, since Jagadhatri is a sustainer of the world, a bringer of motherly love and affection. The idol was being carried through the streets at the time of *Esha*, the last Muslim prayer of the day; and, as it passed by the mosque in Tiljala, some firecrackers exploded in celebration. The worshippers thought, in the silence of prayer, that they were being attacked. They rushed outside and scuffles broke out. Rumours swiftly spread that Hindus had attacked the mosque, and counter-rumours that a temple had been destroyed. That none of this was true scarcely mattered. A detachment of the Rapid Action Force was deployed, and within a short time, order was restored. An incident, which would ordinarily have been insignificant, threatened to become a major communal conflict. We could hear the sounds of tumult from Ballygunge, almost a kilometre away. After midnight the noise died down.

The next morning, this story made headlines in the Urdu press. It went unmentioned in the English-language newspapers, and the Bengali newspaper with the widest circulation, *Anandabazar Patrika*, did not see fit to devote any space to it. In a way, this was the most chilling consequence: for it suggests a separation so complete between rich and poor, that disturbances in the poor areas are not of sufficient significance to be noticed by those untouched by them. The elite remain unaware of – or inexplicably indifferent towards – the combustible nature of the relationship between the two communities in this most secular of states, in which the Left boasts of having maintained harmony and social peace. It suggests how close to the surface old animosities remain. The following morning, the story was the talk of Tiljala Road; but it scarcely leaked out to the majority community at all.

## XXIII
## THE SQUATTER SETTLEMENT

The difference between the Tiljala Road communities and the unrecognised squatter-settlement on the railway track is difficult for an outsider to discern. The distinction is made more difficult by the fact that Tiljala-SHED has tried to extend some of the modest advantages of the recognised slum to the 'illegals', the four or five thousand occupants of the railway slum. When schools and community centres were opened in the unauthorised area, many people in Tiljala Road objected, since they believed the squatters would gain advantages they did not enjoy. While such hierarchies remain among the impoverished themselves, who will bridge the fateful gap between rich and poor?

In an informal school for the children of the unauthorised slum, the work of preparation for 'mainstreaming' is in train. The costs were covered by the Ministry of Women and Child Development until March 2010, but ceased when the Right to Education became operative. Non-government organisations were being invited to set up hostels, to rent homes where schoolchildren can stay and the government would pay for such accommodation. Hostels are supposed to provide accommodation for 25 children, to prepare them for formal schools. When a school has been catering for 200 or 300 children, this will dramatically reduce the role of the non-government organisation, and will leave large numbers of children without access to any education at all. If it seems both perverse and punitive, this is because the Indian government is widely believed by activists to have succumbed to Western ideas of 'development', insisting that formal schooling become compulsory, without regard to the poor children whose education, however imperfect it may have been, will cease altogether.

Tarannum Nabi is 16. Her father is a banana seller, who earns between 100–150 rupees a day (just over $3). There are four girls and two boys in the family. When her father became ill, considerable expense was required for medicines, and so the extra tuition and special coaching she had been receiving stopped. Tarannum believes it is vital for a young woman to get an education before she marries, and for a very practical reason:

> If I can't complete my education I shall be at a disadvantage. I must have a skill to earn a livelihood, because if my marriage fails and I get divorced, or if my husband becomes unemployed, I must be able to look after myself and my children.

There is something admirably prudent, but at the same time, chilling, to see this girl of 16 having to take into consideration that her marriage may fail, long before it has even been negotiated or even suggested. Tarannum's mother has taught her the rudiments of tailoring, but she is unable to practise it for want of a machine. The acquisition of a skill is the mirror-image, as it were, of the dowry-system: if marriage requires a woman's family to provide the man who takes her with money, jewellery and consumer goods, the woman has to provide herself with the means to survive in the event of marital breakdown.

Tarannum does not want to fall into the trap that has caught many women in Tiljala Road, thrown upon the charity of family and the ignominy of return to the parental household. She says she knows the meaning of insecurity and poverty – the long queue for water at the communal tap, the line at the ration-shop which scarcely functions, for paraffin, soap and matches. Tarannum, her mother and grandmother were born in Tiljala. Her great-grandparents had migrated from Orissa.

Tarannum's sister was lying sick with fever in their small house. At any time, it is obvious that significant numbers of people are demobilised by (largely) avoidable sickness. An unhealthy environment – contamination of water supplies and stagnant floodwater, overcrowding, polluted air, mosquitoes and parasites – make for constantly impaired health. The costs of this do not enter the economic calculus, but are borne by the people, whose subsistence is constantly eroded by expenses incurred in the maintenance of their costly poverty.

Tarannum's mother says, 'All she needs is a machine; you can get a second-hand one for 2500 rupees ($50). That will give her security against death or desertion after marriage.' She tells how these houses now occupied by the squatters were illegally built by the 'mafia'. (This word, widely used in India, refers to networks of developers, politicians and their enforcers. It does not necessarily have the same connotations it has in Europe.) They then sold them to the people who have occupied them ever since. The squatters united to chase off the mafia. Although they have had possession of the houses for 20 years, their security is far from assured.

We provided a sewing-machine for Tarannum. When I met her a couple of months later, she had begun to earn a little by sewing – 500-600 rupees per month. She has a Diploma in Tailoring and Knitting, and would like to teach her skill to other young girls. Her parents are agreed that they will not think of marrying her until she is self-reliant. Tarannum estimates 20,000 rupees as a minimum required for a dowry. She is prudent, yet optimistic about her future. If God does not want her to make a stable marriage, she says, she will be able to handle it. She has seen many women divorced, who have no choice but to become maidservants. Sometimes husbands become ill and cannot work; others do not show that they drink before marriage, but afterwards all their money goes on daru. Marriage is a problem, and divorce is also a problem. Tarannum says many girls marry at 15 or 16, because this is a dangerous area and, once girls become the responsibility of their husbands, the parents heave a sigh of relief. They are so concerned that a girl should not get 'spoiled', that they marry her off to a man who creates even more grief. Tarannum is staying with her grandmother in Auddybegan, and she seems to regard this area, on the edge of Tiljala, as safer than the interior. Other girls, she says, are not so fortunate and do not have anywhere else to go. Tarannum is one of many thoughtful and intelligent girls who increasingly have an eye on the long term, and, prudently, do not necessarily regard marriage as a final destination. This is, however, still a long way from abstaining from marriage by choice.

## XXIV
## REALISING THE HOPES OF WOMEN

Salma Khatoon is employed by Tiljala-SHED. Her tenacity and courage are not rare in the women of the poor communities. She lives in a kholabari house, also in Auddybegan. This is the site to which her grandfather came, originally from Barisal which is now in Bangladesh, a town which has sent its migrants all over the sub-continent.

> He came to Kolkata after Partition. There were riots in that part of East Pakistan, and he and several sisters had to run away. My mother came only after marriage. My grandfather worked in a factory which made seat-covers for motorbikes; and my father followed him in the same business. My grandfather came first to Howrah, and then took this house on rent. The landlord is the theka tenant. We only pay 47

rupees a month. There are twelve families in the houses on this site, so if the theka tenant tries to evict us for re-building, we will resist.

When my mother was five years old, my grandfather died. My mother was very young – only in her teen years – when she made a love-marriage. My grandmother wanted my mother to have sons. Every birth was female. She had five girls. One died in infancy, but that left my mother and father with four girls to bring up. That gave them little hope that anyone would look after them when they grew old. Grandmother's wish never came true, but she died with it still in her heart. Before she died, she said to my mother 'As you gave no birth to a male child, I will marry my son to another so that he has a son.'

Salma's father also saw his daughters as a burden. She says,

In this area, boys are not very concerned for their mothers, so you see more and more girls who are taking on responsibilities which in our culture ought to be the duties of boys. My father and his mother did not want to give an education to girls, since it would be of no use to them once the girls were married off. My mother had been educated to Class VI. She had pain in her heart when she had to leave studying because there was no opportunity for her. But she made a resolution that she would give her daughters what she herself had missed. She was a very intelligent woman. To keep the home running, she joined a chit fund and was able to supplement what father earned; her money went on uniforms and books for the girls. It was not much, a few rupees daily. She also started selling clothes, sarees and blouses, going from door to door, and hawking in the market. She would stop at nothing to make sure her daughters got proper schooling. She looked until she found schools that did not ask for fees. At Bhawanipur there was a school for poor girls. She got her oldest daughter admitted, and then pleaded with them until they took another.

When I was in Class VIII, my mother heard of the AIDOS Italian sponsorship programme of Tiljala-SHED. She put forward our names and I was chosen. My father and mother used to quarrel about what he regarded as a waste of earnings. He wanted to take her money, since he regarded it as his. 'Why do you want education? It is not the custom.'

They quarrelled, even physically; and after she died, he tore up all the photographs we had of her. He said it was shameful that his wife should be going door to door, selling clothing. Her reputation would make it more difficult to marry his daughters. Getting sponsorship relieved my mother, and she enrolled my younger sister in school.

While I was in Class IX my mother fell sick. She grew gradually worse. She had gall bladder problems, but her lungs were filling with water, and she spent several months in hospital. I was in Class X when she died. That was 1998, the year I was to do my exams. I failed, but I took them again the following year and passed.

Their mother's death was a catastrophe for the girls. Salma's older sister, Halima Khatoon, decided to renounce her education so that her sisters could continue to study. To do this, she had to acquire marketable skills, at which she showed herself remarkably proficient. She learned embroidery, mehendi, tailoring. She became a beautician and did fabric-painting. She still teaches embroidery and tailoring. From beneath the monumental bed, she takes out boxes with samples of her work – painting, embroidered sarees, designs on silk. She is a woman of extraordinary talent, all of it discovered by the necessity of honouring her mother's desire that her daughters should be educated, and by the sacrifice she was prepared to make for her younger siblings.

Salma Khatoon is grateful to her 28-year-old sister, who, in effect, took over the mothering of the family. Halima Khatoon is a big woman, past her early youth, but the work of her hands, as well as that of her heart, are there for everyone to see.

When Salma passed Class X, many of the family's needs remained unmet. In Class XII, an offer of employment came from Haider Ali, the humane titular head of Tiljala-SHED, whose kindness is belied by his bureaucratic designation as Chief Functionary. With her small salary, Salma was able to take over some responsibility for the education of her younger sisters, Reshma and Shama. Reshma used to work in a call centre for twelve hours a day, as her contribution to the family finances. Salma continued her own studies at Surendra Nath College, an evening college for working people; and although it is not a particularly distinguished place of education, Salma studied History, Urdu and Persian. She says, 'It is not by my work only, but also by the grace of Allah that I graduated in 2006.' She is now doing her Master's degree in Human Rights from the Institute of Human Rights in Delhi. She also did a computer course run by the Kolkata Police and won first prize, which she received from the hands of the Chief Minister.

Both of Salma's younger sisters graduated. One is studying to become a Chartered Accountant, and the other is doing a teachers' training course while teaching in a school. Salma has kept faith with her mother and her older sister, and has herself made sure she passed on her mother's dying wish to the younger girls. Two women sacrificed themselves – mother and Halima Khatoon, and, to a lesser extent, Salma. But the link has been maintained. If their father now likes to take credit for what they have achieved, they do not dispute it.

Shama Khatoon was married in March 2010. The groom works in the South City Mall. The sisters do not observe the custom that younger women must not marry before their elders, for fear that the older ones might become depressed or appear unmarriageable to the outside world. But they do, generally, stay inside the house. They do not mix much in the neighbourhood. But when anybody questions what they have done, Salma says, 'You cannot unlearn what you know; and you cannot reverse consciousness: once you become aware of the world, you will never be ignorant again.'

Halima Khatoon says, 'Most men are looking for a beautiful girl and a handsome dowry. Occasionally, a boy and girl will go to court and say, "We love each other, please write it into the records that we want to marry and we are not immature lovers." You can break free of old traditions, but you can also remain free within your own religion.'

They are not exactly alone, because their extended family lives in the neighbourhood. 'Mostly, they are very conservative, although our father's sister supports us. Poverty makes people reluctant to change. They keep to the old traditions, because that is all they have.'

Just as we are about to leave, Shama arrives, bringing all of the sisters together. It is then time for Salma to go to work. Before going out, she puts on the niqab. This is, perhaps, a sign to the neighbourhood that, although they have become educated, they have not deserted their faith; a gesture of conciliation to what remains a conservative, critical society.

## XXV
## ORDINARY LIVES

Although people do not always tell the whole truth about their lives, they are generally not parsimonious with details: poverty is common property, to which no one has an interest in making a unique claim. In spite of a wide range of economic conditions in the community, from those who have succeeded to those still scratching a living on the edge of subsistence, a sense of shared predicament overrides difference. There is a well-off minority. Alamgir calculates that 5 per cent of people probably earn more than 10,000 rupees monthly. These are owners of property or business people who choose to live close to the source of their livelihood. Not everyone with money moves out; for some, it is a kind of camouflage, to remain among the poor, since no one will suspect they are wealthy. Alamgir estimates that 30–35 per cent of people earn between 2000 and 4000 per month. The greatest number – 40 per cent – earn below 2000 rupees. The poorest are domestic servants, labourers, masons, those underemployed – whether through ill health, old age or lack of skills – and children working in tea-shops, manufacturing units or making wallets or chappals. These are individual earnings: most families have two or three earners, many of them children.

The ambitions of most people are modest: is this a consequence of a culture of poverty and lowered expectations or of a proper humility? Sultan is 20; a handsome young man with copper-coloured hair, a silver earring, white shirt, blue jeans and leather sandals. He looks as though he might be a potential recruit for the mafia. Not so. He is working in a chappal factory, earning 300–400 rupees per week, perhaps double at festival time, and in the rainy season little or nothing. His dream is to start some small business – you can set up a tea-stall for a couple of hundred dollars. He looks forward in due course to being married, to enjoying (this means having sexual relations) and having children. Sultan is frustrated in his attempt to work on his own account. He cannot get a bank loan, since he has no collateral and no one to stand guarantor for him. He is, like most young men in Tiljala, protected against the lure of the mafia and criminality by his faith. He is a strong believer, says namaz five times a day and 'tries to be a good Muslim.' What does that mean? It means, he says, above all, trying to be a good human being. Sultan provided another insight into the nature of poor communities: religious faith, far from leading people into extremism, serves, for a majority, as a moral bulwark against disorder and violence.

We stopped close to a food-seller who has a handcart laden with cooked snacks – *channa*, vegetable curry, *samosas* and sweets. His profit is between 150 and 200 rupees per day, and there are plenty of customers on this Friday morning. Alamgir took a snack from a dish made of leaves. A woman passing by pokes him in the ribs and says, 'It's because people like you eat too much that food prices are going up.' On the corner, a coconut seller with a broad shallow tray has placed a red flower on the slivers of white that are arranged in a symmetrical pattern. He invests 300 rupees a day and makes an average profit of 100 rupees. Here, the area becomes less poor: bougainvillea grows against the wall, trembling with magenta blossoms. The brick houses are neat and whitewashed, and although loops of electric cables cross the thoroughfare, the work is *zari* – embroidery – or the making of better class footwear. There are fine nuances of social standing in poor communities; and many conditions – between modest comfort and destitution – are represented here.

# XXVI
## RECYCLING

You do not have to go far in Tiljala Road before you become aware of the smell of the wholesale recycling units. These are open sheds, with an only apparently chaotic appearance, since each commodity for re-cycling is meticulously sorted. Waste in India is not simply waste: it is known by those who re-cycle it by its market value. This accumulates as it passes through the various stages of collection. First come the children, women and men who are called 'rag-pickers' – both a descriptive and disparaging term, according to who uses it. They sell immediately to the 'retailers', who sort it and sell on to 'wholesalers', who then pass it in bulk to the 'stockists', from where it goes to paper mills, glass or plastic factories, foundries and smelters. Although this Tiljala enterprise is a wholesale unit, it employs labourers to parcel up the goods, men paid 60 rupees ($1.30) for a twelve-hour day. Some, who have no family here, sleep among the waste; and they take on some of the characteristics of the objects of their labour – unkempt and neglected, ragged, exhausted like the used-up objects they process.

The rate paid to those who collect the waste is fixed at 1 rupee for a kilo of paper, 2 rupees for plastic, 50 paise (half of 1 rupee) for a kilo of rubber, 50 paise for a bottle if it is not broken and 1 rupee a kilo for broken glass. A kilo of iron is worth 5 rupees; plastic toys fetch 12 rupees a kilo; plastic water bottles 4 rupees a kilo; aluminium 50 rupees a kilo; brass 60 rupees; and copper 100 rupees.

Rural habits die hard in these urban areas, which began as provisional settlements for temporary migrants. A surprising number of people get part of their living from livestock. A woman walks by with a headload of tiny chickens in a wide bamboo basket covered with fine-meshed wire. You can hear them, a faint music of small birds issuing from her head. A few grubby geese scavenge among the rubbish in the streets, overseen by a little boy of about six with a thin stick in his baby hand. A cockerel is tethered by a rope to an iron post, straining to escape and flapping its bronze wings; a child is minding a goat on a chain. Only the dogs, ubiquitous and mangy, whose sustained howling is part of the sounds of the settlement, belong to no one.

## XXVII
## SKILL AND AMBITION

Not all the work is as elementary as that of the chappal-makers. In one small windowless unit, Mohammad Kaishan, 22, is working for an optical manufacturer. His unit is adding magnifying power to glass for spectacle-making, by treating it both chemically and by grinding. Mohammad Kaishan earns 150 rupees per day (about $3). The owner of the unit receives 4 rupees for every pair of lenses: 60 per cent of the work is done here, the rest is carried out in units elsewhere. The finished product goes to a number of companies, including Modern Opticals in Kolkata, and from there, all over the world. Mohammad Kaishan works at the rate of 60 pairs for 100 rupees, and a 12-hour day guarantees him the 150 rupees.

It is highly skilled labour. A high-watt bulb in a tin throws an intense light onto the rough work-surface. The circles of plain glass are imported from China. The glass is sanded and held fast in an iron circle. A wheel, operated by a handle, spins inside a pit, and this pressures the glass, which is ground to the magnifying power required. It seems incredible that such refined products should be produced in these makeshift conditions. Mohammad Kaishan says that apprenticeship and guidance of many months are required before the worker becomes proficient; and this is strange, because most of the workers are younger than he is: many little more than boys. Zeeshan, the next eldest, is 16. Mohammad Kaishan is working in his spare time to gain his Bachelor of Commerce degree. He has four brothers, one of whom has already graduated. His father died three years ago, so he is the principal family earner. They have to produce faultless work, or it will not be accepted. Mohammad Kaishan has a double responsibility – to his impoverished family and to the company which provides a livelihood, and which has a high-tech image that is far removed from the crude circumstances in which their high-specification products are made

The next building shelters a more typical, cruder industrial activity: an ancient iron machine is cutting cardboard ready for packaging. Islam, 14, has been here for two years. He operates a handle, shiny with use, that chops lengths of cardboard to be folded into boxes for consumer goods – television sets and refrigerators. He earns 300 rupees per week ($6). There are four brothers and two sisters in the family. One brother is working with him and another in an adjacent cap-making unit. Islam never went to school. His father used to work re-cycling leather scraps, but he has now become old and does not work; in any case, the leather industry has been moved away, so he can no longer travel to do the work. Islam works 8–10 hours a day. It is monotonous, repetitive work, but what else will he do, since he has had no education and possesses no other skill? The aggregate income of the brothers allows them to survive, and the indivisibility of families is the basis on which this remains possible.

A small street of low cramped houses faces a high brick wall, along which washing hangs on a plastic cord. Outside the first house, a woman dressed in black is cooking rice over a clay stove. She is Kasida Bibi. Her husband, who plies a cycle-rickshaw, is not working because he has been sick. His 70-rupee daily income has gone, so she has come back with her three daughters to stay with her mother, Saida Bibi. The house has two rooms, with a low door; height is so restricted it is impossible for an adult to stand up inside. Saida Bibi's husband is a ragpicker, earning 60–70 rupees a day (about

$1.50). They pay 40 rupees per month for the house, which is little more than a brick hovel. In the back room there is just enough space for one bed. Shelves around the wall are crammed with vessels, buckets, clothing and other household necessities. Nine people share this house, but they cannot all lie down at the same time, so the children sleep on the footpath when it is not raining.

Almost every other hut in this row is a small factory. Some are making the plainest rubber chappals, others fancy footwear with beads, sequins and spangles. Most confirm their earnings to be around 150 rupees for a twelve-hour day, but the income is not reliable. When orders in one workshop dry up, the workers move elsewhere. One young man says he has worked in at least 30 different places in the past two years.

Bupen Sada has been in Tiljala Road since 1965, when it was still a rough ramshackle settlement. An old man of 82 with white stubble and a faded lungi, originally from North 24 Parganas district, he left his village to find work in a factory in Kolkata. He was employed by the Bengal Waterproof Company for 36 years and retired in 1995. He received no recognition of his years of service and no pension. He had four children, three girls and one boy. His son was killed at the age of 21 in an accident; he was struck by a lorry in front of Mother Teresa's home. One of his girls lives in Chennai and he lives here with a second daughter, her husband and their five children. The eldest of these is a young woman who works in Shanti Dham, a refuge for the mentally ill. Bupen Sada says his Christian name is Lawrence: he converted as a young man, but has never really practised his adoptive faith. He says that over the years not only has Tiljala become more crowded but people's behaviour has also deteriorated. 'Children no longer obey their parents. They may be earning, but they are addicted to drugs or solution or liquor. What guidance will they have for the future?' His wife died in 2000. He says that long life is no blessing here, since it means you lose everyone you love, and must depend on the charity of your children.

## XXVIII
## THE EXPLOITED

In a chappals unit next door, a boy sits on a stool feeding soles into the mouth of a machine, which treats them with a chemical so that the adhesive that attaches the upper part of the shoe will stick. He receives 3 rupees per dozen pairs of soles, and earns 100 rupees a day. He is 14, and his name is Meraj. He works twelve hours a day. He never went to school, and indeed, is handicapped – capable, his companion says, of doing only this repetitive work. The labour is also dangerous. Meraj is covered with a silvery-grey deposit from the chemical with which the machine sprays the soles: his clothing, his hands, his hair and face are covered with what looks a silvery cosmetic, make-up for some grisly charade. Only the whiteness of his eyes and his artless smile in his beautiful, vacant face; inhaling the life-destroying substance for twelve hours a day to help his family. He has two brothers. His father works in a machine-stamping press, but he drinks and beats his wife. He lives in Topsia, and makes the half-hour journey each way on foot to save money. His family occupies one of the shanties I had seen in Topsia a few days earlier.

## XXIX
## THE URDU GIRLS' SCHOOL

On the edge of Tiljala Road, near Auddybagan, is a narrow concrete building, with wire mesh windows and shabby curtains to keep off the sunlight. Inside there is an affecting scene: about 20 young women, aged between about twelve and 18. They are sitting at cramped school desks, the antiquated kind in which the seats are joined. All are wearing the same uniform – cream-coloured salwar kamiz and a red shawl. This is the only Urdu-language school for girls in this part of Kolkata. This may seem unremarkable, but given the low priority of the education of girls and the fact that this school is in Tiljala, its existence is itself a small miracle.

The school has been here for a quarter of a century. It has never been recognised by government, nor received any funding. It was originally built by the United Bustee Development Association, with the help of a Dutch agency. The electricity bill is paid by the UBDA. Apart from that, it is self-sustaining. The girls pay 30 rupees per month, and this is the source of the 'salary' of the three teachers who work for a monthly wage of about 300 rupees ($6) each. They teach up to Class X. The mothers of the girls are maidservants, vendors, their fathers rickshaw-drivers, tea-shop workers or chappal-makers. This school belies the fatalistic assumption that the education of girls is of no interest to Muslim parents, since it involves incalculable sacrifices on the part of their families and of the girls themselves. They learn Urdu, English and Bengali, Maths, History and Science. There is no other Urdu school within several miles, and it offers the girls a safe place in which to study.

All work to earn the money that pays their fees. Most work at home, making chappals, paper bags and embroidery, while some visit neighbouring middle class areas as maidservants. Their dedication is reflected in the devotion to the school of the three teachers, Shakila Khatoon, Shahida Khatoon and Rizwana Parveen:

> We have been struggling for 25 years, but we are still surviving. We applied for recognition to the government for support, but we do not know the fate of the application. This is not the first time we applied. Three years ago, we were told our application had been lost.

The government has funds for minorities, but it chooses to withhold them, especially from Urdu schools, perhaps because they believe – falsely – that Urdu speakers may be dangerously pious Muslims and because the government of West Bengal advertises its secular credentials, it may be reluctant to fund such an initiative.

The building is cramped and sparsely furnished. A folding door separates a small partition for the teachers' office, in which there is a metal desk, a clock and a big chest of drawers in which papers are stored. Pinned to the walls are some blue and orange crepe-paper streamers, covered now with dust. This is a remainder of Teachers' Day, on 5 September, when the girls decorated the school to show their appreciation of the women from whom they have received so much.

I met some of the girls. Razia Sultana was born in Tiljala. Her father cannot work because he lost a hand in a meat-cutting machine. She has a brother who does embroidery work and earns 500 rupees per week (about $11). Razia lives with her uncle and gives tuition to younger girls to pay her school fees. She also helps with the domestic work in the household. She dreams of higher studies, and is sad that her family was broken by her father's accident. Razia is 18. She wants to learn computer skills and sewing, in case of the failure of marriage. I was surprised by the number of far-sighted young women who have taken such an eventuality into account. It is not that they expect it, but they know they should prepare for any contingency. All the girls have seen so many marital tragedies where the women have come to grief, and grief has certainly come to them. Her uncle – her mother's brother – is looking for a husband for her. She does not say it, but her wish to follow her studies stares out as deeply from her dark eyes as if it were written there.

Zeba Anjun is 15. She too has lived here all her life, with her mother and father, an uncle and three sisters. Her father is an electrician, who arranges lighting for parties and marriages. He also erects arrangements of decorative lights in private houses. He earns 100 rupees per day. Her uncle makes slippers and draws 500 rupees per week. Zeba herself makes the uppers for the shoes, working two or three hours each day. She spends that money on school and extra tuition and coaching – which costs her 200 rupees per month – because she is anxious to succeed. She wants to be a doctor, but knows this requires long and arduous training. She admires and loves her teachers, because they have opened her eyes to a wider world; she also knows they give their service almost free of cost, and this places her in their debt. Zeba, in her turn, wants to make sure a new generation of girls also has access to what she has learned. She says most girls go to government schools because they charge no fee, but there is also often little learning either. One of Zeba's sisters is married, another is also studying here. Her parents are anxious for her to develop her skills for later in life, but also, she says candidly, to enhance her understanding of the world.

She talks freely of relationships with boys. It can happen that girls have affairs with boys and when this becomes known, marriage hastily takes place. But in such cases, there are often disputes over the dowry. Resentment builds up and quarrels take place even before the marriage is over. The reputation of girls is at stake. Reputation – *izzat* – is a matter of family honour. If there is any scandal, it will ruin the reputation of the whole family. Zeba dreams of a world in which young women can have their freedom, in which trust between people overcomes superstition. Marriage should not be the only destiny for a girl.

With their dazzling smiles and independence, the girls at this unrecognised school ought to be models for the whole of India; instead, they barely survive, and then only through the commitment and duty of a handful of teachers. This obscure place ought to be a place of pilgrimage to those who see Muslims as backward and unconcerned with education. The girls in the Urdu school are determined to rise above prejudice and ignorance – and not only of the minority community – to take their rightful place in the world. It is, perhaps, the site of greatest hope in Tiljala; an obvious fact which is, apparently, lost upon those who sit in authority in Kolkata and West Bengal.

# 6
# Victimisation

Milan Molla, his younger brother Deedar, and his cousins Ramzan and Shaqib were scavenging the banks of the Hooghly in August 2008 when they unearthed a shell that had apparently been abandoned in the river. They carried it home to their small house in Cossipore, where they tried to break open the unexploded ordnance. The market value of the metal would offer a significant windfall to the family. Milan owns a small tea stall and sometimes deals in scrap metal, which was why the discovery of the unexploded shell was seen as such a stroke of good fortune. As they were trying to open the casing, a shattering explosion occurred in which Deedar, Ramzan, Shaqib and their great-uncle Hasan were killed instantly. Milan was elsewhere when his family tried to dismantle the weapon: his absence from the scene saved his life. The entire family, shocked and disbelieving, was plunged into panic and grief. Such a tragic occurrence naturally had to be reported. The Commissioner of Police and senior officials visited the site of the blast. They immediately declared that it had been an accident and had nothing to do with terrorism.

There the matter would have rested, but, three days later, a group of policemen from the department that tracks criminal activity in the Port area descended upon the stricken household. They evidently thought it would be a good idea to implicate the bereaved young man in a false charge. They raided his house and took Milan Molla to a post belonging to the Special Staff of Port Division. There, he was told that he would be charged with causing an explosion, the accident that killed four members of his family. He was offered an alternative to this grim prospect. If he gave the police a sum of 1.5 lakh rupees (about $3,000) he would escape being booked for 'terrorist offences.' Milan is illiterate. He was not in a position to measure the power of the police. Although it was obvious he had been involved in no such activity – he had not been at the scene when his relatives tried to dismantle the bomb – he had no knowledge of his rights, and word was sent to his mother informing her of the situation.

Anwara is 50 years old. She, too, was scarcely a match for the police conspiracy. 'What else could I have done?' she asked. 'We were still in mourning, shocked by such a loss when they came to pick up my son.' She borrowed 35,000 (about one-quarter of the police demand) as a first instalment – 10,000 rupees from Milan's wife's father and the rest from a local trader. Within a couple of days she had paid the money to one of the police officers.

Anwara started a vain search for the remainder of the ransom. It was not until about a month later that a political leader of the CPI(M), Mohammad Salim, was visiting the area. Some local residents informed him of what had happened, the police action, the kidnapping of an innocent young man and the promise to release him on payment of a sum which few people in the area have ever seen. Mohammad Salim immediately alerted the highest police authorities, who said they would look into the matter. The Police Commissioner – who had announced that there was no criminal activity involved in the blast – met the family. The following day the boy was released.

Two officers of the Special Staff of Port Division went to Milan's house the next day, and asked the young man to withdraw his complaint against them. 'They said they would return the money my mother had paid, if I withdrew my complaint.' Milan refused to rescind his complaint, particularly in view of the promise of the Commissioner, that justice would be done.

In late September 2008, Milan and his mother were invited to go to the Port Office to meet the Deputy Commissioner. There, they identified the man who had taken the money from Anwara. The deputy reassured him that action would be taken against those who had mistreated her son. But Milan remained fearful that, by way of revenge, they might involve him in another false case, since such experiences are familiar to everyone in poor Muslim communities.

The Commissioner of Police told the press that the inquiry was ongoing; and that 'if the officers were found guilty, they would be punished.' Six months later, despite police assurances that the money would be repaid, Milan and his family had heard nothing. The officer identified as the culprit who had framed Milan, was being investigated, to discover whether he had taken all the money, or whether colleagues had also been involved.

The Additional Commissioner of Police, who led the inquiry, said that he was not responsible for the return of the money that the policeman had extorted from the family. He was reported as saying, 'Departmental proceedings are under way. I don't know how the money will be recovered, even if he is proved guilty. There is a separate procedure for that.'

The money was not returned. The fate of the corrupt policeman is also not on record. It appears that no one has been disciplined. The bureaucracy can absorb its own wrongdoings, and those who are on the receiving end of the illegalities of the forces of law and order have no redress against the injuries they have suffered.

# 7
# Tangra

Tangra is another 'forgotten' place, or perhaps a mis-place, for it lies on low land, divided in two by the same turbid canal that sends its turbulent waters through Topsia. It too has a history. It was originally a settlement of Hakka Chinese – the earliest Chinese settlement in Bengal, which dates back to the early nineteenth century. The first trading post was set up at that time at Diamond Harbour. The Hakka came from the coastal areas of China, where Guangdong, Fujian and Jianxi meet. They have been traditional migrants, carrying their particular culture – especially cuisine – with them. But their principal activity was in the tanning industry of Kolkata, processing and exporting leather goods; it reached its highest peak of prosperity in the first half of the twentieth century.

The community has declined over the past 30 years, since many people have emigrated – to the United States, Britain and Canada. The highly polluting industry was moved to Bantala by the government of West Bengal in 2007, and although some illegal units remain, they have no future here. There are still Chinese-owned tanneries, but in recent years, the area has largely been deserted by the original owners; and the main monuments to Chinese dominance are two or three schools, and the houses of the dead in the extensive cemeteries beside the canal; while the undead – the Muslims of Tangra – who have replaced them, now perform much of the re-cycling of the city. The Hakka lived in Kolkata without friction or violence. Indeed, after the disturbances in Kolkata at Partition and again in 1964–5, there were few communal disturbances, and none involving the Chinese. The CPI(M) prided itself on its secular record; at least until the time of the demolition of the Babri Masjid at Ayodhya in 1992, when the Muslim slum in Tangra was burned to the ground.

In December 1992, people took shelter, ironically, in the Tangra slaughterhouse. A refugee camp was set up nearby and today is an open space, still known as Relief Camp, that is the site of much of the recycling of the city of Kolkata.


I

THE TANNERY


Although the tanneries of Tangra are supposed to have been removed, not all have gone. For one thing, people complain that the Bantala site lacks the infrastructure to deal with tanning, water and power shortages. Many Chinese businesses have taken their capital and abandoned Kolkata for Canada, Britain and Europe. The estimate of the numbers of Chinese still in Tangra is only 3–4000, less than a tenth of those who lived here 40 years ago.

We took a winding lane into the heart of Tangra. On either side, the grey concrete bulk of old tanneries and warehouses. A significant number of these – particularly if they front the main road – have been turned into Chinese restaurants. This is gentrification, Kolkata-style. Some buildings are too derelict or inaccessible to be used for other purposes; others are still used as industrial premises. Young men wheel carts full of skins, dyed Krishna-blue, through the streets and the feral smell of hides pervades the air; the accumulated redolence of a century of skinned creatures clings to walls and pavements.

In a great half-open barn-like structure we met Faiz Ahmed, who treats hides and prepares them for the factory. His brother-in-law purchased the tannery from a Chinese owner who has left the country – a plaque on the office door announces that this was the Chiu Lee Tannery, although it has now been re-named Mumtaz Tannery. The skins, sent by dealers in Rajabazar, come here to be split, that is, the layers of skin separated. The business is illegal, and will, sooner or later, have to move; but for the moment, the local police are happy to allow it to continue at a price. Faiz Ahmed's brother-in-law has already moved the greater part of his work to Bantala.

The process is simple. The raw leather – which has already been dyed – is very stiff. It is placed into huge rotating drums full of heavy rubber balls which, as the drum moves, strike against the leather, softening and making it more supple. The thud of the balls against the metal machine maintains a continuous thunder-like rumbling; their rise and fall helps the drum to turn. It is a fairly rudimentary technology, but very effective. When the leather is ready, it is passed through machines – made in Thailand and China – which tears apart the thick skin. Each skin is split into its four or five separate layers, so that it attains the particularly pliable texture appropriate for export, mainly to France and Germany, where it will be made into high quality gloves. Some of the material stays in Kolkata, and provides the leather for small purse and wallet-making units.

The 20 or 30 workers in the tannery are from Bihar. Many also sleep here. It is difficult to calculate the numbers of people who sleep in their place of work: one consequence of the reduction of the city space occupied by poor people's dwellings is that many have found alternatives – some of which are no improvement on the vanishing slums: people sleep in taxis or in garages for rickshaws; on verandahs and in cellars of buildings in which they serve; in factories and industrial units; or they are stacked vertically in high-rises.

Sleeping in the tannery saves the migrant workers money. They are paid about 2500 rupees a month. The environment is desolate: a metal shed on concrete pillars, stone floor and a corrugated metal roof. Part of the yard is open to the sky. Everywhere are piles of skins, spread out so that they look like two-dimensional versions of the animals they once were. Scraps of leather litter the yard. The labourers are Dalits. Unmesh Paswan has ten people dependent upon the money he sends home. He has no expenses apart from his contribution to the fund with which they buy food. They have no holidays, and the bleak streets of Tangra are all they know of the city – rather than broadening horizons, the urban environment often closes them down. Instead of rice-fields, fishponds, trees and sky, their world is reduced to concrete and stone and the materials of their labour.

'Sometimes', says Faiz Ahmed, 'the police come and seize the material, take it to the police station. Then I have to pay a ransom on it. The police demand 20–25,000 rupees for release of the leather, but since they have nowhere to store it, they will let it go for 2–3000 rupees. The customary "rental" to the police is 3000–4000 a month.' At his brother-in-law's bigger factory at Bantala 400 people are employed. Only some of the preliminary processing (dyeing and splitting) is still carried out in Tangra.

Faiz Ahmed regards his personal position here as only temporary. He, like the business, will move on. He is preparing for a degree in Business Studies and will start his own company in the same line; not because he is particularly drawn to tanning, but because this is what the family knows. His office is also a bare utilitarian place with a metal bench, stools and bare walls, ornamented only by a picture of his brother-in-law receiving some award or commendation from Buddhadeb Bhattacharjee.

We went one day to Bantala, to where the tanneries have been removed. It is a vast estate covering hundreds of acres, a flat treeless expanse, where new buildings – by no means all of them tanneries – are rising in what look like the beginnings of a new city. Wide spaces separate the buildings and these, in turn, are segregated from dormitories and quarters for the workers. The estate has a perimeter fence and three official entrances. It is like a city under quarantine, some medieval plague-stricken settlement, although the smell of death is only that of animal pelts, being unloaded from trucks – the hairy rind of creatures recently living, around which cluster haloes of dancing green flies. On our way back into the city from Bantala, we were stuck behind a small truck, loaded high with skins that had already been treated, and dyed a pale bluish colour. On top of this precarious cargo a young man of no more than 19 or 20 years old was sleeping, sprawled in an attitude of utter abandon, hides piled beneath him, like the sloughed off husks of an infinite number of his past incarnations.


## II
## THE RESTAURANT

Tangra is also a lesson in the mutability of things: a location traditionally associated with the most polluting of industries can be transformed into the site of smart restaurants and eating-houses, where the wealthy of Kolkata come to dine, be seen and hold business meetings – a metaphor for a whole city that is in a state of epochal upheaval and change.

We walked back through the twisting lanes filled with the dusty smog set up by each passing vehicle. There were an unusual number of wild dogs, attracted perhaps by the remains of food from the restaurants. It was just before the Chinese New Year. A Chinese newspaper – the last in Tangra – occupies part of a one-storey building of what used to be the Tanners' Association of Tangra. Two men were translating from the Bengali press, laboriously recomposing in Chinese characters yesterday's news. They are too busy to talk to us. We visited the school – an extensive structure with a broad verandah on the three sides of an imposing square building. Some elderly Chinese men who were playing cards could tell us nothing about the history of Tangra, but say we should meet Monika Liu, who runs the Beijing restaurant, the most exclusive and prestigious in Tangra.

The restaurant occupies a large plot of land that used to be a timber-yard. It has glass doors with pale panels of glazed lime-green images of a Chinese garden and dragons – Chinese designs executed by Bengali craftsmen. The interior is cool, spacious and scrupulously clean – a not uncommon contrast in Kolkata, where an outer appearance of neglect and decay frequently conceals a modern and superbly finished decor. We sat at one of the tables, set for lunch with white tablecloth and stainless steel cutlery; we ordered fruit juice and told one of the waiters we would like to see Madame Liu. We were not expecting very much, if indeed she deigned to see us at all, since we were strangers to her and had made no appointment.

It was an agreeable surprise when Monika Liu joined us at the table, a capable business-like woman in her 50s. She placed her mobile phone on the white tablecloth, and our conversation was punctuated by frequent calls. Monika also carried an epic story of loss and dispossession, but also of triumph over adversity. It is not only Muslims who have, at one time or another, been victims of cultural estrangement. Monika's father came to India from Guangzhou (earlier known as Canton) during the Japanese war against China in the 1930s, and her mother was a refugee at the time of the 1949 Revolution. Her grandfather remained in China, and during the years of famine under Mao, he retreated to the forest, where people had to eat leaves off the trees; just as during the Second World War, her mother's family had also taken refuge in the jungle to avoid Japanese bombs.

Monika Liu was born in Shillong, where her father had a grocery store. She was one of five brothers and sisters, a child when the Indo–Chinese war broke out in 1962. This was for them a catastrophe, since the whole family was immediately interned in Assam and imprisoned in Naogaon jail. 20,000 Chinese were arrested at that time. Later, they were sent to a camp in Rajasthan. Monika was then eleven years old. The family spent more than five years in the camp, not because they continued to be enemy aliens but simply because the authorities had forgotten all about them.

'My childhood was stolen', she said. As the eldest, it was part of her duty to look after her four siblings. She remembers her mother constantly weeping.

> Tears were always running down her cheeks, and I wondered what made her so inconsolable. There were schools in the camp and I learned to write English, although I could not speak it. The war was soon over, but we were left in the camps. We were of such small

account that no one bothered to inquire into our fate. I was 16 in 1968 – the time at which I should have been learning and exploring the world was spent behind barbed wire, and for no good reason. I wrote to the Home Minister of Rajasthan, asking him why we were being detained and what crime children under 16 could possibly have committed that they should continue to be interned for years. He actually visited the camp and, shortly after, we were transferred back to Assam and then released. All our property had been confiscated; but when we arrived at the bus station in Shillong, I remember a crowd had come to greet us. The family was split up, and we had to stay in three different houses. We had nothing.

After what happened to me then, I ceased to be afraid of anything. I feel I have died once already, so nothing else can frighten me.

I was sent to a school run by the Assemblies of God, where my English improved rapidly. My mother started selling *momos* [Chinese savoury rolls] which she made and sold outside the school; and I could say that was the beginning of my career in the restaurant business. My father took a shop on rent. I was married in 1971, and that is when I came with my husband to his tannery in Kolkata. Before I knew what had happened, I had a child, and I began thinking 'What am I going to do with my life?' I was not one to sit and look at the walls, so I started a restaurant, the Kim Ling, here in Tangra. I can truthfully say that I was instrumental in giving the people of Bengal a taste for Chinese cuisine. The police used to recommend my restaurant to their own personnel and to visitors. If the police did anyone a favour and they were asked what they would like in return, they said, 'Bring us some food from Kim Ling.' I now have five restaurants in Kolkata. My youngest son runs the one on Park Street.

In the 1950s, there were more than 40,000 Chinese people in Kolkata. We used to have two Chinese newspapers, but now there is only one, a flimsy reprint of articles from other papers. The community has gone, dispersed across the globe.

Madame Liu frequently visits China, and although she recognises that China is far more developed than India, she regards Kolkata as home.

> In India, people are known by their caste. China knows no such distinction – everyone there is regarded as equal. Life is good in China's cities now. But I could not live there. China has grown so fast. Women can retire at 50 and men at 60. I stay with my Auntie, and she gets a pension which is the equivalent of 7600 rupees a month (about $150). But whenever I am due to return to Kolkata, my heart beats a little faster.
>
> I am sad to have seen the decline of Tangra. 50 years ago, there were over 200 tanneries. In the 1960s, young people started going to Canada. They said they were going for a holiday, but they never came back. Then, when it became more difficult to get a visa for Canada, they started going to Europe, Austria, Sweden and Denmark. When the government ordered the tanneries to close, many took their money, especially small and medium-sized leather works, and decided to invest their capital abroad. Chinese society here is only the ghost of what it was.
>
> People have become less honest as they have become better off. Sometimes Chinese people on official visits to Kolkata ask for me to make an inflated bill, so they can claim it on expenses. I never do that. People in India are more honest than the Chinese. But we are alike in that both societies are basically conservative as far as family values are concerned.
>
> My work is my life. If I go away on holiday, within a week I want to be back working. I would be lost without it.

Mme Liu insisted that we have lunch in the restaurant, and refused to take any payment. The restaurant began to fill up – mostly with well-dressed business people, mainly Bengalis, but there was also a party of Europeans and a group of Chinese visitors in suits. Although Monika Liu's family had been mistreated by the Indian authorities, this was a result of neglect and bureaucratic oversight rather than the systemic distrust and denial of its Muslim minority.

It was a shock to go out into Tangra after the cool serenity of the restaurant; and a surreal contrast.

## III
## THE CATTLE YARD

We went in the direction of the Tangra slaughterhouse and stood beneath an arch where white lettering on blue tin stated it had been founded in 1869. The original building is still there, crumbling, painted yellow, without windows, but with slats in the wall that release the odours of blood and death. A new construction has grown up alongside, more modern, coloured a dark sienna. The street leading to the slaughterhouse is crowded with cows and buffaloes being driven to their death; a continuous stream of grey and beige animals, some with elegant horns, driven by young men wielding lathis to keep them from straying. They are taken from the cattleyard – an open space about 200 metres from the slaughterhouse, where they have been brought by businessmen from all over West Bengal and beyond. Between 700 and 800 cattle are slaughtered daily, except on Thursdays – the eve of the Muslim holy day. We spoke to the chief veterinary inspector, who is appointed by the West Bengal government to ensure that only healthy animals are sent for slaughter.

The sights and smells reminded me of my grandfather's small slaughterhouse in Olney in Buckinghamshire in the late 1940s: he told the story of how farmers used to come in the middle of the night to beg him to slaughter a sheep or a cow that was sick, before it died of natural causes, since it was then forbidden to be used for human consumption.

The vet admitted that the same thing is common here today: people are in a hurry to have ailing animals killed; and it is part of his job to make sure that sick or diseased animals are not passed as fit.

In the cattle yard boys were playing cricket among the cowshit and the pervasive animal smell. Sheikh Panchu was supervising the transactions that take place before and after the animals are killed. A man in middle age, he has been working here for 18 years. His work is to collect the money from the buyers and to deposit it in the office until the transaction is complete and the animals have been slaughtered. Retailers come to buy when the animal has been killed – a cow will be cut into four pieces, and each small retailer may take one piece. Shiekh Panchu works 22 days a month and earns between 200 and 250 rupees daily.

The boys driving the cattle also retain an aura of the farmyard, a faintly rural air in the middle of the city: their hair is neglected, their clothing wornout and shabby. Some are barefoot, their trousers smeared with cattle dung, a broad engaging grin of youth whose carefree business it is to drive dumb beasts to their death. Mohammad Nasir is about 19; he concentrates on maintaining the cows on the straight path to the slaughterhouse and has been working since he was a child. He earns 300 rupees per week from each of the three or four businessmen whose cattle he conveys to their place of execution, making sure that the carcasses are indeed those which belong to their proprietor. He exudes the healthy indifference of youth to the fate of the creatures that will within an hour be killed, skinned, dismembered and dispatched from here to the Muslim meat retailers of Kolkata.

And indeed, emerging from the slaughterhouse, there is a steady procession of cycle-vans, their cargo covered with bloodstained sacking, which take the animal parts to their destination. One boy labours up the incline from the slaughter-house, his muscles and sinews straining as he pedals a heavy load of the heads of cows; glazed eyes, tongues protruding, the foam of saliva hanging in viscous loops, raw at the spot where they have been severed, dripping blots of dull crimson into the dust. It is as though he is conveying away the evidence of a terrible crime; which of course, to Hindus, it is. Others are carrying the flanks and limbs of creatures, legs protruding through the metal bars, the semi-translucent grey horn of the hooves kicking passers-by on the crowded road. The smell of carnage makes people cover their mouth and noses, as the roughly-dissected animals are taken to markets; even though meat remains out of reach of the income of the poor.

A group of *hijras* – large-boned, middle-aged, with heavy traces of facial hair – hold their saree in front of their face as they hail an autorickshaw. What have they been doing in this place? I asked. They smiled but did not answer. They are sex workers; lumbering and inelegant, their lips vivid scarlet, dust and mud staining the lower part of their clothing, this is perhaps one of the few places in Kolkata where they can find customers – among migrant men living in isolation, squalor and garbage, a smell of death in the air. Here, perhaps, desperation for contact and sexual release is not squeamish about its – ambiguous – object of desire.


## IV
## THE URDU BOYS' SCHOOL

Almost opposite the entrance to the cattle yard, on a yellow-painted building with peeling walls, a scroll announces an Urdu-Medium Boys' School, established in 1926. The building was destroyed during riots at the time of Partition and subsequently replaced. 'There have been many riots in Tangra', say the teachers, 'in 1947, 1964, 1971 and 1992.' The entrance to the school is at the back, so there is no outlook onto the cattle, the lowing of which is scarcely – together with the cries of the drovers – helpful to learning.

400 children are enrolled in the school, which is recognised by the West Bengal government; although 'recognition' is evidently a distant one, since the first thing you notice is the almost total absence of amenities, the dereliction of the building and the meagre educational resources at its disposal. The building itself suggests indifference towards those who are fated to receive instruction within its cheerless walls.

Mohammad Nezamuddin is the head teacher. He is a serious man dedicated to his pupils, but has no illusions (it would be impossible to work here if he harboured any). He says,

Educating the poor is no easy task. Nearly all the children work – shoemaking, collecting garbage, recycling rubber, ragpicking. The daily attendance is between 200 and 250, that is, just above half those enrolled; and you should remember that these are five- to nine-year-olds, children generally thought to be too young for the labour market. Most work after they finish school and are also expected to help with chores at home. Some assist their mothers who work as maidservants. Often, the fathers cannot meet the family expenses; and many drink, some because they are irresponsible, others because their own labour is so exacting. They are rickshaw-pullers, cycle-van drivers, labourers in leather or plastics factories.

A more unsuitable site for a school would be difficult to imagine. It is unhealthy, exposed to dust pollution kicked up by the hooves of the animals, noise and smell. There was no drinking water in the school and no toilet facilities until two years ago. The children suffer from fevers, tuberculosis, diarrhoea, asthma, breathing problems. The teachers say that eleven *kattas* of land have been allotted for a new school, but that is next to the slaughterhouse and even if it were to be constructed – a distant prospect – it is unlikely to be in more salubrious surroundings.

Mohammad Nezamuddin says, 'We daily eat poison, but are inured to it. At least we do not live here all the time as the children do.' He lives near Sealdah. His family originated in Bihar. They have never visited his place of work. His daughter has finished her Bachelor of Arts degree in English, Bengali and Political Science, and his son is at Francis Xavier School doing his Higher School Certificate. He wants to be an engineer. They enjoy a modest well-being, but whatever effort the headmaster makes, he cannot make good the long-term privations and neglect of those with whose education he is entrusted: home, working and environmental conditions are all obstacles to effective work.

A more desolate place of learning would be hard to find – the peeling walls, damp, concrete floor, grey metal cupboards and wooden table, and clock with spindly Roman numerals and cold white strip lighting. In this, it was like many educational establishments we saw, the austere bareness of which mockingly echoed the deprivation of the people they serve. That this should be regarded as a *refuge* for children says a great deal about the circumstances of their lives. It is lunch time. On the wooden table, the provisions which the teachers have brought from home: plain wholesome fare, perhaps, but far beyond anything the children will be eating today. Before we go, the headmaster asks us if we know of any source of funds to provide even basic facilities for

the children – private or charitable – because there is little
likelihood of any official financial help.

V

THE JUNKYARDS

As we go down towards the canal, great bales of recycled
materials litter the landscape. Narrow streets, godowns,
small houses are stacked with waste, piles of debris against
walls, in open spaces, under rusty corrugated iron sheds and
in windowless brick workshops. The area is stacked with
shiny woven-plastic bags, jute sacks and packing cases, which
give the impression that the whole suburb is on the verge of
some epic evacuation and has packed its shabby belongings in
preparation: a world awaiting collection. Tangra is a visible
outlet for the waste of Kolkata's growing consumer society,
whose used-up merchandise comes to be recycled. The people
are also victims of a prior triage, because the great majority
are Muslim.

Many of the units where material is sorted are highly
specialised. They are open to the street, so that women
and men crouch atop vast piles of waste – plastic, paper,
cardboard, rusty metal. Three women squat on a mound
of what look like coloured ribbons, so that it appears that
they have an embarrassment of material for preparing festive
decorations. This is, on closer scrutiny, tough plastic tape,
used for securing bundles and packages of goods. It fills
a whole rickety metal warehouse with its multicoloured
tangle. The women must cut the knotted and twisted tape
into lengths that can be melted down and re-used. They sit
with a menacing curved blade on a wooden stand in front

of them – the kind of implement used to cut vegetables – to slice the tape. Each day they earn between 50 and 60 rupees, but work is not always available, and pay is irregular. Sometimes the factory owners do not come to collect the material, or they delay payment to the owner of the unit. Hasina and Hamida from North 24 Parganas district live and sleep among the waste. Both have been deserted by their husbands, and this is the only work available to women with neither skills nor experience outside the home. They have left their children with other family members and return to the village only when they have an enforced holiday. Jehanara, who is younger, lives nearby and goes home at night. They do not count the hours of labour: they are bonded to the capricious schedules of waste which arrives unpredictably.

In a dingy shed opposite where the women work, a deafening, vibrating machine is chopping up plastic goods into small pieces ready for re-use. The shed has wooden rafters and a tiled roof, which rattle with the violence of the machinery. It is bare and dirty, with a small opening in the brick wall at the back for ventilation. There is a thin partition just inside the open door, with a concrete floor, where the male workers can wash the plastic dust from their bodies. The men must work as long as the machine continues: it is a primitive instrument, a rectangular metal trough, into which the plastic objects are fed, and which crushes them and spits them out through a funnel at the base, filling the air with tiny motes of plastic. The workers labour twelve hours a day, earning between 100 and 150 rupees. The young men – about 19 or 20 – do not pause, as they take up more plastic objects from the pile that fills about half of the shed – a stack of ancient plastic colanders, bowls, dishes, buckets, containers, canisters, dispensers, bottles – which they cram into the mouth of the voracious machine. Sanju, from South 24 Parganas district has been bathing. He ties a lungi around his waist and comes out from the noise to speak. A man in early middle age, he has been working here for many years. He has nine children, three of whom are working. He sleeps here at night, and goes home one day a week to take his wages and see his family. He has, he says, no health complaint, despite the inhalation of plastic dust not only during his twelve-hour day, but at night also. How can he sleep in such an atmosphere? The answer is obvious – fatigue.

Mohammad Kabir Rahi, an elderly man with a grey beard and faded lungi, originally from Uttar Pradesh, speaks of the night in 1992 when Tangra was razed to the ground by angry mobs in the riots that followed the demolition of the Babri Masjid at Ayodhya. His family lives in a small hut, which looks as though it has been excavated from the mound of the waste materials. He has three daughters, but two are already widowed, victims of existential, as opposed to wilful, desertion. The husband of the third daughter works, recycling plastic. One daughter is a maidservant. The total income of the family is between 2000 and 2500 rupees a month ($40–50.) There are five children in the small one-room house, eleven people in all, sharing congested space and an inadequate diet. Mohammad Kabir worked for a non-government organisation in 1992, and he helped save people from the violence that seized the city. He believes the government is not really concerned about the minority Muslims, except at election time. The family has a ration card, but no Below Poverty Line entitlement. Mohammad Kabir's wife also works as a domestic, and sometimes brings leftover food from her work-place.

Tangra has the air of a great labour camp, in which the people have been compelled to repeat endless tasks of penance with no hope of redemption. This is also the penultimate destination of the material collected by the waif-like 'ragpickers' – the 'stockists' who sell on to the recycling units, the mills and factories.

The whole area is pervaded by the feral breath of tanneries and the mouldy scent of used up goods. Some by-products of slaughter are also recycled here. The intestines of cows and buffaloes are used for sutures and stitches in hospitals, for wounds and operations. In a chetai and metal structure with a concrete floor, metres of voided gut lie in pinkish filmy coils. It seems scarcely credible that the product that goes from here winds up with a transnational company, but this unit is run by a sub-contractor – or sub-sub-conractor – to Johnson and Johnson in Mumbai. Sub-contracting is a labyrinth in which relationships of oppression are hard to trace, since they lose themselves in vast no-man's-lands of concealment.

Here, the raw materials are chemically treated, in preparation for the next part of the process. Because animal gut is both malleable and biodegradable it is ideal for the purpose. Lengths of translucent intestine lie across the concrete floor. There is a well in the hut, with a plastic bucket, with which Mohammad Amin constantly cleanses the gut of all traces of blood and other extraneous matter, and keeps the floor clean. Mohammad Amin is from Bihar. He lives here in the unit, accustomed to the smell of damp and dead animals. Once or twice a year he goes home to Bihar to see his wife, his two boys and one girl, who survive largely thanks to the 100–150 rupees he is paid daily. He works up to 16 hours a day, because there is nothing else to do, and the work is without end. The slaughterhouse sends the material daily, and

when he has cleaned and treated it, it is packed for delivery
for the next stage in processing. After that, Mohammad Amin
has no idea where it goes, or how it finds its way to the final
beneficiaries. It is, he says, a lonely life, but not as lonely as
a life without livelihood.

In another structure animal intestines have been distended
with air until they appear as long hoops of monochrome
balloons on bamboo poles protruding over the canal, as
though in readiness for some sombre carnival. These will
eventually serve as casings for sausages.

In the next unit, men are weighing cardboard for recycling.
On each of the cardboard panels is stamped the exhortation
'Be Good To Your Maruti'. The owner of the godown is
working with the men. He pays 20 paise per kilo for
cardboard, 50 for plastic, 20–25 for scrap paper, 50 paise
for plastic bags. He is from near Patna, but has moved his
family to Kolkata. They do not live in Tangra. The labourers
are paid 120 rupees per day and work ten hours from 8 a.m.
until 6 p.m. They do not sleep in the godown.

Nearby, a small shed is half-filled with glass, on top of
which squat two women. This glass mountain rises from half
a metre or so near the opening of the shed to about two metres
against the back wall: bottles, broken fragments, shards
and jagged splinters of glass. The May sun dances on the
promiscuous glittering of crystal, dazzling the eye like light
playing on water. The two women are Amma Khatoon and
her daughter, who segregate the different coloured glass and
separate unbroken bottles from the shattered pieces. Outside
sits a little girl of about ten, Amma Khatoon's second child,
and she throws to her all the green glass that passes through
her hands. It is a compelling spectacle, women and glass
that winks and glimmers like a cavern of precious stones.

Each woman earns about 20 rupees a day for handling these objects, the reflections from which illuminate their faces and fingers with spots of white leprous light, while the deadly beauty of glass dust sparkles in the air they breathe.

A young boy wheels his cycle-van over the rickety wooden bridge that spans the canal. He is collecting broken and abandoned footwear. He separates rubber or plastic from worthless substances like cardboard or cloth for sale; he is lucky if he gets 70 rupees a day. The water in the canal is thick and greenish, bubbling up to the surface in places, where the gas breaks wind in a sulphurous smell. On little islands of rubbish in the water, a surprisingly green vegetation of thorn-bushes and water-hyacinth, with junk, shreds of clothing and plastic caught in their spiky branches. The boy is delivering the worn-out footwear to the site where they will be taken apart and the material made ready for re-use.

## VI
## UNMAKING SHOES

If shoes are made in Tiljala Road, they are unmade in Tangra. Against the high yellow-painted wall of a factory compound are piles of shoes, perhaps two metres high, spilling over the sidewalk onto the road. At the foot of each small mountain of shoes, boys and men are working. They tear apart each item and separate the different components. These small acts of destruction form a poignant contrast to the labour of those assembling the same items in Tiljala Road. It seems the journey is short from manufacture to dismantling – perhaps a measure of the perishability of cheap footwear, but also a comment on the feverish labour that uses up workers who are as readily replaceable as the items they make and destroy. Wooden heels are set aside to be sold as cooking-fuel. Rubber is placed in one pile and plastic in another, ready for melting down and re-use. The workers earn between 100 and 120 rupees for a twelve-hour day. It is scarcely imaginable as a human activity, this tearing apart of discarded and used-up shoes which are still pervaded by the smell of feet. Mohammad Shahid is in his late 30s. He lives nearby with his wife, mother-in-law and four children. Two of his children go to school. Women and girls collect the shoes from the municipal dumps and sell them here. Mohammad Shahid pays 3.5 rupees per kilo, and then sells the sorted materials directly to recycling factories at 6 rupees per kilo. An average daily supply amounts to 500 kilos.

The factories pay either every 15 days or monthly, although half is withheld to ensure no interruption in the flow of waste. Mohammad Shahid is from Bihar. He has worked here for ten years. Because this is a public footpath, he has to bribe the police to be allowed to pursue his work in peace. His three sons are working here; they are ten, twelve and 15 years old. They had to stop their education, because dowry-money was needed for his daughter's marriage. Once they had ceased, they did not return to study. The marriage has taken place, although he does have another daughter, who is studying in Class XII – a rare example of female privilege. But for the boys no such exemption is allowed. Work, he says grimly, is a jealous taskmaster. In any case, what is the point of education, when livelihood is here – he points to the banks of shoes against the wall. There will be no shortage of work as long as people walk in shoes. The boys labour on, impassive, without pause beneath the overseer's gaze of their father. What they think of an indefinite prospect of tearing apart shoes for ten or twelve hours a day for the rest of their working life they do not say; indeed, do not – perhaps dare not – think about.

## VII
## WASTING PEOPLE

In the small lanes between the godowns is a market, where basic foodstuffs are sold. The ground is wet from recent rain. The people in the street also share their dwellings with waste. We met a man beating his son with his fists, a boy of about twelve. The child was writhing on the muddy ground and screaming. The neighbours watch. A second boy hands the man a stick, the more effectively to thrash him. The father is shouting that the boy is ruining him by neglecting his business. A young man explains to us, 'The boy is not very clever. He has some mental handicap.' All the more reason not to beat him. The father pauses, his eyes flashing with anger. He lowers the stick. 'Only because you are here', he says, 'I will show him mercy.'

In a small brick hut, a man and woman are recycling batteries, taking out the lead for re-use. The work is abominable: in the hut, the air is thick with lead dust. Outside stands a great heap of the coloured cylinders of torch and radio batteries, which have been gutted of their re-usable components. The colours of these containers – blue, red, green, orange create a splash of brightness in the gloomy afternoon, with its swollen rainclouds and evaporating water rising up like ghosts from the puddles on the path. Sheikh Ibrahim comes outside; a man in his late 40s, inclined to fat, wearing a dirty lungi and covered with lead-dust, his hair streaked grey with lead. He wears a bandage around one leg to protect a wound from the poison. He earns 60 or 70 rupees a day. He has six remaining children. Two have died in the past year, within four months of each other. These brief biographies pass between people, not to elicit sympathy, but simply to inform one another of the changing – and often deteriorating – condition of their lives.

In Kolkata, it seems, everything is saved to serve again. Plastic cups are now widely used for tea, replacing the little clay mugs which were endlessly recyclable. The plastic cups, although almost weightless, are worth 16–18 rupees a kilo. A boy of about ten has a sack almost full of them. This is the result of two days' work. It weighs a little over two kilos.

The only thing wasted is the people; their energies, their health, their dignity. It is, perhaps, the most eloquent comment on a society of consumption that humanity should also be consumed, without regard or pity; and the truly savage irony is that they should be sacrificed in a vast work of the conservation of inert matter.

Just when it seems that nothing could be more desperate than the efforts of people to re-cycle the most trivial object or wornout material, it appears that there is someone even more wretchedly scavenging a kind of living from the city waste. The vast municipal dump to the east of Kolkata provides further opportunities for the retrieval and re-processing of waste. Each day the city garbage trucks dump quantities of rubbish that has previously escaped the watchful attention of collectors. This is sorted by another army who rescue and re-package discarded goods; and it brought back into the city, where it provides livelihood for the urban village of Mathpukur – each kholabari house surrounded by sacks of plastic, glass, metal, rubber and any other debris of even minimal value, waiting to be dispatched to the wholesalers.

The waste of Kolkata is much traveled; like the individuals who reclaim it. But they pay a high price, as the incidence of wounds to feet and hands, cuts, eye and skin infections attest.

The dump – which now covers many acres – has, over the years, been leveled and transformed into vegetable gardens. The organic waste serves as a powerful fertiliser, but the toxic and inorganic components also enter the food chain. Rows of red and dark-green spinach, cabbages and gourds rise out of the ground. Fragments of glass, metal and plastic remind that this scene of rural tranquility has risen out of contaminated urban waste. 'Dhapa' cauliflowers – that is, those grown on the dump – are famous for the creamy-coloured foam of their florets. The effect upon the bodies of those who consume them has, so far, not been assessed.

## VIII
### MEDICAL WASTE

Sitting on a piece of sacking beneath a high yellow wall we met Vicki, who was separating metal needles from plastic syringes. Beside him is a heap of hospital waste. Patiently he tears out each needle from the transparent container.

Vicki is 18, already a veteran of medical waste having worked here for more than five years. He is paid 100 rupees a day. He lives with his mother and one sister in a small hut of chetai in nearby Malikbazar, a hovel for which they pay 300 rupees per month. That is the sole extent of their expenses, since the hut is without electricity or water.

Vicki's father died two years ago. He was a rickshaw-puller addicted to daru. Vicki is unusual in this neighbourhood, because he is Hindu. He works a twelve-hour day, and knows that the work is hazardous – the needles have been contaminated by bodily fluids, infections and other contaminants; sometimes they draw his blood too, but so far, he has suffered no ill effects.

Vicki wears grubby nylon yellow-and-black shorts, a T-shirt and has a thick ring in each ear. He had his ears pierced in Newmarket, and bought the earrings for 50 rupees each. He says, 'After I have finished work, I rest and then go out with my friends to have fun in Newmarket or Dharamtalla. We drink fruit juice and sometimes stronger liquor.' He says proudly 'When I go out, no one knows who I am. The real Vicki is not here. I have no shame in my work. My friends work in markets or malls. I become another person when I leave here. This is not me. I am not my work. I am Vicki. I make myself.'

He takes us to his house. It is a thin, poor structure, among a huddle of self-build huts just off the main road. Vicki's family eat twice a day, roti and banana, rice at night. The police come from time to time to destroy their house.

In the small housing cluster some neighbours gather. Zubeida Bewa's husband died of a heart attack. She has three daughters and one son, and she runs a small tea-shop. She was born here, but the family, originally from Bihar, are now all dead, and there is no further connection. Her 'tea-shop' is a tin box on stilts, which sells tea, bidis and confectionery. It earns her just enough to keep herself alive with the grace of God.

Vicki is working for a small company that collects medical waste from nursing homes, private and government hospitals all over the city. The owner of the company was the only person I approached in Kolkata who refused to talk to me. He asked, 'What is in it for me?' I said, 'Nothing.' 'Then why should I talk to you?' 'There is no reason why you should.' He had once spoken to a journalist from an international newspaper, who published a story about uncontrolled hazardous waste, and this had caused him problems with the authorities. The outcome was that he had to pay a significant sum to the police to be allowed to continue his dangerous calling in peace.

## IX
## INHERITED DISCRIMINATION

Among the recyclers of plastic twine used for tying up packages and bundles of goods, I came across Mohammad Nizamuddin, standing in front of the rough shelter in which he conducts business. He is 55. He was wearing glasses, and if he had a studious air, this was because he is a highly educated man. He studied to become an engineer, and after graduation, he sat the examination for a government job. He passed easily but was offered no employment. He gave tuition while patiently waiting for employment in government service, but when nothing came, he started this business of plastic processing. He made a living to ensure that his children should get a good education, even though it had been of small use to him. His son studied diligently, passed all his examinations, gained a Bachelor of Science degree, First Division. His daughter is also in the second year of her Bachelor of Arts degree. He has one other son and a daughter already married. But he now finds himself telling a sad and bitter tale of inherited discrimination, because his son, too, has been unable to find work and is now going through the same experience as that of his father 30 years ago. What a disincentive it is, he says, for Muslims to educate their children! Muslims are constantly being accused of being indifferent towards education. But when they give the lie to this assertion, they are, more often than not, excluded from the work to which their qualifications are supposed to entitle them. Mohammad Nizamuddin has despised the labour he has done all his life, but submitted to it in the hope that the world would be kinder to his children. He sent his son to Mumbai, so that he could get work in the Gulf. There, he was cheated by an agent who promised a job in Dubai; but he paid money and the agent disappeared.

> After graduation I had no work, and now my son is going through that same sense of rejection. The government of West Bengal is indifferent to the position of Muslims. They do not care. They have taken our support, and given us nothing in return.

This story is repeated daily in the Muslim communities of Kolkata; and now that power really is slipping away from the CPI(M), this is certainly a contributory factor to its defeat: a third of a century has been long enough for a new generation to know discrimination and rejection under an administration unchanged in all that time.

## X
## THE TANGRA FIRE

On the canalside in Tangra, a fire gutted about two hundred homes in January 2010, leaving about 1500 people homeless. The shanties are highly flammable here; not only are they made of wood, chetai and bamboo, but many also store waste which is dry and combustible. Fires in poor communities are common; and fire spreads even faster than the rumours about how it started, whether it was arson, accident or negligence. If it was accidental, there is no great eagerness on the part of the householder to admit it, since this will make her or him unpopular with neighbours. In the vacuum of knowledge, stories are spread. It may have been instigated by powerful people who want the land. Perhaps it was revenge. Maybe government has caused it – after all, playing with fire is something of a political occupation in Kolkata.

Such events usually pass without comment, since they are one of the acknowledged hazards of the slums. This time, it was different. Elections were scheduled for later in the year, and the competing political parties were quick to offer help. Non-government organisations and charitable institutions swiftly followed. New building material – of a far higher standard than that of the previous structures – was brought to the site. Political philanthropists came forward with clothes, utensils, household goods and food, so that the afflicted were overwhelmed by an embarrassment of compensatory gifts; an inspiration and encouragement, one man said, to arsonists all over Kolkata. The scene, six weeks after the event, was one of highly active reconstruction: with regular bamboo frames, tiles for roofs, the new homes will be more ample and generous than anything that stood here before. The general opinion is that it was an accident: the government has no interest in claiming land which still has so little value, although they have been dredging the canal to make it flow faster. One day, perhaps, it may become a stream of clear water, in which case the canalside would be a desirable location. But not for a long time yet.

We met Dilshad, a smiling young man of 21, who had lost his rented workshop in the fire, and finished goods worth more than 30,000 rupees. All the displaced people have been promised a new start in the re-made community; although many are asking why it took a fire in election year before they could expect half-decent housing.

In the meantime, Dilshad has moved back into his house. He invites us into a three-storey concrete structure. It looks ancient, with its drift of dust accumulated in corners, its scraps of cardboard and fabric from the work done here, but is only five or six years old. Humidity and heat stain everything they touch. The entrance is at the side of the building, and after climbing two crumbling flights of stairs, we penetrate into the deep dark interior, a long unlit passage with a smudge of daylight at the far end. There are doors on both sides of the concrete corridor. The door to Dilshad's house is open. There, in the first of the three rooms the family occupy, he has set up his work, a long bamboo frame, with a length of material, taut and ready for embroidery, temporarily stitched to the bamboo edge.

Ten people live in the house: Dilshad's mother and father, five brothers and three sisters. His father has a plastics business, recycling material from old water and sewage pipes. His brothers work in plastic and rubber factories. Dilshad studied in a madrasa to Class V. He left school at twelve and was apprenticed to his brother-in-law, already skilled in embroidery work. His sister and a young boy are seated behind the frame, stitching beads onto the motif of flowers and birds already stencilled onto the fabric. It is intricate and laborious work. Heaps of tiny beads lie in hollows at the centre of the material. The workers scoop up eight or ten of these with a needle and, with a deft stitch, add a centimetre to the outline of a peacock's tail, a flower or an elegant silver leaf. The sister is working with shorter beads: the needle pecks at the miniscule aperture in the crystals, which are then swiftly incorporated into the arabesques of the pattern, which springs to vibrant life beneath their proficient touch.

Each piece of work – mostly shawls – yields about 2000 rupees. It takes ten days to complete. In the shop it will sell for at least 5000 rupees. It is always a marvel to observe objects of such mastery and beauty which come out of these dismal surroundings. Old skills are tenacious. It is an irony that those who campaign most vigorously against child labour would find themselves bereft of some of their most treasured possessions if their wish were to be fulfilled, since it is to the nimble fingers of children that the accomplishment is communicated. For children to be versed in craftsmanship is no punishment, although to be compelled to labour excessively most certainly is.

Dilshad's mother is proud of what he does. She came from Bihar after her marriage. They still have relatives there, and visit from time to time. There is peace and fresh air in the village, but it is Kolkata that provides them with livelihood and the promise of a better life.

Dilshad's friends gather in the street. Salauddin works in the slaughterhouse. He does not kill the animals, because that is a highly skilled job, but he cuts up and weighs the meat and prepares it for sale to retailers. He is a tall, sensitive-looking boy; and it is difficult to associate him with the dissection of carcasses. He says he does not think about it; only about the 600 rupees he earns weekly. Shahnawaz has just left his job in a wallet factory. He was earning 2000 rupees per month, for an eight or ten hour day. He left because the money was not enough. He quarrelled with the owner, out of pride. He thought it was an affront to his dignity to work for so little.

The boys say this is the third fire in Tangra in the last few years. It soon became clear that there are other ways than in the accumulation of flammable materials that these communities are combustible. What change do you notice, I was asked as we passed along the row of shanties. I could not detect a difference until I observed the image of Ganesh in a small wayside shrine. We had now come to the Hindu slum. There is an invisible frontier, unmarked, but known to everyone. It is, perhaps, marginally less squalid than the area we have passed through, but the first thing we see is identical forms of labour: a family of young girls cutting out plastic lids for perfume bottles. The stoppers have been made by machine in great strips, and it is their work to cut each piece out with clippers provided by the factory. They are paid 1 rupee per 100 pieces.

I met Dilshad a few months later. He had had a quarrel with his family and as a result had taken an overdose of sleeping tablets, which required hospital treatment. He was slightly embarrassed, but said that everything was all right once more. He is clearly a more troubled young man than he appears; sensitive, anxious to be helpful to others. On this occasion, he was going to visit a family who had come to Kolkata to see their daughter, who was in hospital. They had travelled from a distant village, and knew no one in Kolkata. Dilshad was going to see the girls' parents, to tell them where they could stay in Kolkata as cheaply as possible and to make sure they were not cheated in the city. He said his mother had gone to Bihar. Neither he, nor any of his brothers and sisters, has the slightest wish to go there. For them, Bihar is ancient history, even though the language and culture still inform their lives.

## XI
## THE CHINESE GRAVEYARD

Just behind the canal is a now virtually disused Chinese graveyard. It is an open field, with weathered dark grey tombs, slabs of elongated pock-marked stone, as though commemorating a race of dead giants. A man is sleeping between the tombs, while boys play cricket in the dusty space where grass grows in the monsoon. On the steps leading down to the burial ground sits Bibi Banu, in a blue and yellow saree, holding a tiny grandson in her arms. Her broad face, which looks as though it were made for smiling, is a picture of shame and sorrow. Just behind her a young man is shouting, waving his arms and dancing as though at a wedding; an incongruous image in this solemn place. He wears a gold earring and dark blue kerchief tied around his forehead. The children gather round him, laughing, mocking. He is Setoon, the 18-year-old son of Bibi Banu, and he has been drunk since morning. He dances around the graves, pretending to be animated by the spirit of the dead Chinese, gabbling in a plausible mimicry of the language; his appalled mother is afraid that he is dishonouring the dead; fearing, perhaps, that the slight to their dignity may be avenged. Setoon says he can also speak English, and then speaks nonsense with an English accent. The little boys look on with wonder and a little apprehension, but the laughter of the older ones is derisive.

Bibi Banu's husband died many years ago, and she had to bring up her children alone. She could never have anticipated the vexation this boy would cause her. Her eyes fill with pained resignation when she looks at him, since she feels a humiliation of which he appears unaware. He thinks the children are laughing at his performance, but it his drunken condition that amuses them. He is addicted to drink, and his mother knows that is no laughing matter. The grandmother clutches the baby to her body, as though to defend it against the lost pride of a son, who is himself little more than an adolescent.

The family lives in the graveyard. They have constructed two brick rooms in a corner of the cemetery; clumsy masonry, concrete floor and wooden doors, with a wall in front to shield them from the sight of the graves, and perhaps from the spirits which hover, unappeased, around this neglected place of repose. Sheikh Nasim, brother of Setoon says there are few funerals now. He is an unofficial caretaker, and although he receives no pay, he makes sure the burial ground is kept clean and is not used by drug-takers. People come here to rest – he points to one or two elderly men sleeping between the tombs. The living of Tangra are trapped between the dead, the moribund canal and the treeless dust.

The family survives by cutting away superfluous rubber around rings that will be fitted onto fans for car engines. The rings are joined together in great sheets, and must be separated one by one. They work together and earn between 100 and 150 rupees a day between them. Sheikh Nasim fetches the material from the rubber factory and they sit on the threshold working as long as the natural light lasts. All five adult members work, but Setoon is unreliable. They sometimes give him money for drink, for fear that he may otherwise steal. Bibi Banu feels the abasement of living in the cemetery, among the dead who, may soon enough claim her wild son for themselves.

Two months later, we met Bibi Banu again. Her son was not at home. He had told his mother he is working, but she did not know where. Bibi Banu was now concerned with the marriage of her daughter, Soni, who is 20. She said the wedding will cost '1 lakh of rupees'. This was probably a figure of speech – it seems unlikely that such a sum will ever accrue to the family in a lifetime; what she was saying is that it would cost a great deal of money. We gave her 200 rupees, which she tucked away into her saree, disappointment clearly visible on her face.

## XII
## A DIVISION OF LABOUR

Leaving Tangra, we saw an elderly man, sitting cross-legged in front of a stone on which were piled small oval strips of leather. With a machine, he was punching a hole at either end of the leather. What are you making? These, he said, will be tied to pieces of elastic for making a sling or catapult. It is for killing birds. I looked up at the empty skies of Tangra, from which, apart from a few crows, the birds have already long vanished. If ever there was more vain labour, it would be hard to find it in this wilderness, abandoned by all but the most desperate creatures on earth: the people.

## XIII
## RESERVATIONS

In February 2010, the West Bengal government announced that it planned to reserve 10 per cent of government jobs for 'socially, educationally and economically disadvantaged sections among backward-class Muslims in the State.' A similar proposal had recently been struck down in the courts in Andhra Pradesh, since reservation based on religion is against the Constitution. The West Bengal government said it was stressing the three secular yardsticks, so that it should avoid the prohibition on affirmative action on religious grounds. Until now backward-class Muslims had to share a 7 per cent quota kept aside for Other Backward Castes.

Within this limited category, a definition already exists of 'backward Muslim sections', although on examination these are seen to be arbitrary and there is little evidence that many Muslims have benefited from provisions that already exist. The occupations appear to have been chosen at random and, what is more, they are for the most part, a direct transference to Muslims of a Hindu classification of what constitute backward occupations – weavers, butchers, construction-workers, landless cultivators, barbers, religious mendicants, pillow-makers working with cotton waste, mountain-dwellers, fruit and vegetable sellers. There are two categories which even the government was unable to define. Nobody even knew what '*chowdhulis*' or '*patidars*' are. Imran tried to find someone from each of these occupations, to ask them if they knew of any beneficiary of such quotas. He found representatives of all the groups (none had benefited from the reservations policy) except the last two, which remain undefined, and apparently undefinable by anyone in a government which is supposed to administer their special privileges. The only person he met who might conceivably take advantage of the proposed arrangement was a washerman, an honours graduate who had applied for work under the 7 per cent reservation quota. He had applied – unsuccessfully – as a teacher. He was now running a laundry and dry cleaning business.

Apart from him, most Muslims were either unqualified for government jobs, or have already acquired other skills, inappropriate for official employment, in leather working, embroidery and chappal-making. A majority are illiterate, so at what level would they enter government service? The government is vague and evasive, since they have no data with which to work. They had done no research or preliminary work. In any case, disadvantaged groups have to acquire a certificate to state that you are from Other Backward Castes, and Mohammad Murtaza, the laundryman, said he had been trying without success to obtain his certificate for 15 years. The general feeling was that this was an electoral ploy, to appeal to Muslims in the abstract, without practical consequences or advantages. In any case, the great majority of poor Muslims in Tangra, Topsia and Tiljala Road had not even heard of the government's policies, since they live in a world apart.

## XIV
## THE MUSLIM GIRLS' ORPHANAGE

The Muslim Girls' Orphanage in Ripon Street, although it offers shelter to girls from all over West Bengal, is home to a disproportionate number from Tiljala, Topsia and Tangra. It is a four-storey building painted blue-grey, with Qur'anic verses prominent on a high pediment. Rifat Faridi is superintendent, a stern but humane woman, whose family is in Delhi while she lives in the orphanage. There are 230 girls in eleven dormitories.

The idea of 'orphanage' is a sad one, as indeed it must be, but this institution is not quite what it seems. Most of the girls here have no father, but the mothers of a majority are living. They have sent their girls to this retreat because, they fear, they are unable to look after them – with all that implies of guarding them against premature sexual intentions in the slums and settlements where they live. Most mothers are maidservants, living in middle class households, and they feel their daughters are more secure here than they would be if they tried to look after them in a room in an unsafe area. The mothers are allowed to visit their daughters once a month, since to do so more frequently might disturb the girls in their studies.

The orphanage takes girls from the age of five and keeps them until marriage, which is not permitted before they are at least 18. The institution receives many proposals for marriage for its girls. The reasons for this are complex. There may be a perception that girls brought up in this kind of seclusion will be docile and obedient. It is certain that will have had no previous experience of sexual relations. They may also be regarded as potential good earners, since they have studied well. Indeed, the young women exemplify the real gender problem in Muslim communities, which has not to do with 'empowerment of women', as many non-government organisations declare, but with challenging male supremacy. Society is sustained by women. Theirs is the real work, and without them, the communities would be in a state of advanced dereliction.

Proposals received by the orphanage girls are always thoroughly scrutinised, and the life of the young women is monitored after they leave to get married. Most marriages, says Rifat Faridi, are successful. 'We receive more applications than we can deal with. At the moment we have no girls of marriageable age, but the proposals continue to come.'

Girls can choose whether to attend Bangla, Urdu or English-medium schools. About ten per cent go on to higher education and reach Bachelor of Arts level. Rifat Faridi asks if we would like to speak to some girls. She sends for Wardah Parveen, who is twelve, a serious slim child in pale blue school uniform with white blouse. She speaks a modestly fluent English and gravely expresses her desire to become a scientist. Her parents were migrant workers in Saudi Arabia, but her father was killed in a road accident and her mother remains in the country as a maidservant. Yasmin Abbas is a year older, a more mature girl in a hijab and floral dress. Her mother is also a maidservant, in New Alipore in Kolkata. Yasmin's favourite subject is Physics. Both girls say they have an intellectual advantage over those who live at home, since there is time and space for study; the effects of this seclusion on their emotional development are, of course, not a subject for discussion. Wardah is proud of her knowledge of English, and would like to recite a poem. She begins, an English-medium classic from W. H. Davies:

> What is this life if so full of care,
> We have no time to stand and stare.
> No time to stand beneath the boughs
> And stare as long as sheep and cows.

The existence of the orphanage offers a number of unspoken comments on poor Muslim society – the fear of mothers for the protection of their daughters, which makes them think that parting with them will make them safer and give them a better chance in life than a biological parent can. The orphanage protects them against child marriage and sexual exploitation. It also confirms that the childhood of girls remains a lesson in marriage as destiny.

The Superintendent insists that the responsibility of the orphanage does not cease at marriage. She has involved herself deeply in the lives of the girls for the past 13 years, and she often weeps at their weddings. The girls continue to consult staff for advice, and are counselled if there are problems in the marriage. They are given no dowry, but a gift of jewellery is made. Girls who have left come and go freely, offering help and serving as role-models to younger girls.

The Orphanage, then, is, apart from offering asylum to bereaved and unprotected girls, also a metaphor for the vulnerability of girl-children, their exposure to early marriage, assault and social disgrace. It has a quasi-parental role, but is also a powerful indictment of male dominance and egotism.

## XV
## BEYOND SLUMS

Is it only poor Muslims in India who are experiencing a growing sense of estrangement, or does this represent a wider sentiment? During the course of our time in Kolkata, we met a number of Muslim university teachers, journalists, non-government organisation activists and politicians. Many of these, too, said they were made to feel as if they were interlopers in their places of work, even in higher professional posts. This was especially true of teachers of Urdu, Persian and Arabic, but it also affected people in newsrooms and common rooms where assumptions about Muslim stereotypes are an unexamined part of daily discourse. Often, indiscreet remarks – about illiteracy, the size of Muslim families, polygamy, the prominence of religion – were usually followed by the disclaimer 'Oh I don't mean you', or 'You are different.' But Muslims reported that they often felt disregarded, or were looked at in a way which mutely interrogated their presence in this seat of learning or that college. It is surprising that places of higher education should also not be exempt from the dominant prejudices. A professor of Persian said there is little personal interaction between Hindu and Muslim staff:

They have a background among the bhadralok. I am from Kidderpore, and the feeling is that somehow I have no background. They also patronise me, because of an attitude that my subject has no worldly value. 'You are teaching them to be unemployable.' There is no significance in what I teach. The implication is that we are partly responsible for backwardness among Muslims.

The same man also said how difficult it is for educated Muslims to mix with the poor. He said insecurity is the key to the sense of Muslim apartheid:

Insecurity accounts for all the things Muslims are blamed for. We who are educated occupy a particularly painful position; since we are cut off from most poor Muslims, and we also do not participate fully in the social life of the majority Hindus.

He reported that a colleague said to him,

... 'You have been in Kolkata so many years, and you cannot speak Bengali.' ... My family were from Bihar, my father was a worker in Calcutta Port. We lived in a slum, but he managed to educate me. I gave tuitions to help pay for my education, and got my degree in Persian. I studied at Maulana Azad College. I am made to feel – subtly, but quite clearly – that I do not belong.

On our walks through Muslim areas we came to Taltala, where a CPI(M) office was recruiting members. A row of red plastic chairs below a banner which fluttered in the breeze and advertised the philanthropic and revolutionary achievements of the CPI(M). Here we met Bablu, a prominent party member. He wanted to make sure we knew he was not parochial: he had spent time out of India, four years in the United States, and in Britain where his brother is studying. He owns a significant amount of property, and has a fruit wholesale business. He says,

> I am well off, I don't deny it. Many people are puzzled why I should belong to the Communist Party. Normally, it attracts the poor and downtrodden. But I believe in its rules and regulations, I think it has the right idea for the development of society. As a Muslim, I recognise all it has done for Muslims in West Bengal. After all, there have been no riots since the CPI(M) came to power, except in 1992, and they would have been much worse if any other party had been in government. Muslims are able to open businesses – you look around this *mohalla*, most of the small shops are Muslim-owned.

Many people observed that the CPI(M)'s boast of what it has done hardly amounts to a reversal of the exclusion and poverty of Muslims in the city. 'We stopped you being killed, and we didn't prevent you from setting up businesses. What kind of a record is that after a third of a century in power?'

We talked about Shah Rukh Khan, the film star whose film *My Name is Khan*, had been an object of controversy in Mumbai, where Bal Thackeray of the Hindu chauvinist party, Shiv Sena, had threatened a boycott. Shiv Sena had branded him a traitor, when he said there was no reason why Pakistani players should not be included in the Indian Premier League cricket teams. During the auction for players for 2010, no player from Pakistan was selected. It was Shah Rukh Khan's comment on this that led to the controversy. The actor stood up to Bal Thackeray, and cinemas in Mumbai, nervous at first about political violence, finally showed the film, which proved a great success.

Bablu says the ban and the hype was all part of a publicity drive. It is business. His movie will simply make more money. 'It will be a big hit. He is a friend of Bal Thackeray. The film cost 60 crore [6000 lakh] to make, it will net more than 200 crore [20,000 lakh]. Shah Rukh Khan knows only money and fame.'

There is an interest in Khan in Kolkata that outstrips his role as the 'king of Bollywood.' For he is the owner of the Kolkata Knight Riders cricket team. And he has struck a deal with the Todi brothers to publicise their brand of underwear, known as Lux-Cozy. His players will promote the product. The Todi brothers are believed by many to have been implicated in the apparent suicide of Rizwan in Tiljala, who married the daughter of Ashok Todi. Many Muslims feel that this form of 'integration' of Muslims into Indian society occurs most smoothly only where big money is concerned, especially in the shadow-zone where corruption, violence and show business meet. This is, of course, closed territory to poor Muslims.

We went to the Aliah University Building, a splendid pillared edifice from 1827, a soaring structure of red brick and yellow plaster, with Doric columns and inside, an arcade with Ionic columns, high stone corridors and echoing rooms. Originally founded by Warren Hastings in 1780 as the Mohammedan College of Calcutta, it was popularly known as Kolkata Madrasah College. Its status was changed by the West Bengal government in 2008. The Madrasah College was dissolved in

a controversial shift that demoted its traditional curriculum
– teaching Arabic, Persian and Muslim jurisprudence, history
and theology – to a single department, while at the same
time, introducing degree studies in English, Economics,
Journalism and Mass Communications, Business Administration. This was in response to 'the needs of society', according
to the government, which saw an opportunity to integrate
traditional and modern attainments in a predominantly
Muslim university. The students protested, sat on *dharna*
and occupied the red-brick Victorian hostel opposite. Some
saw the move as an attack on specifically Muslim culture,
although the authorities insist it is an attempt to build upon
Islamic traditions of scholarship in preparing young Muslim
men and women to cope with the evolution of technology
and knowledge-systems of the contemporary world. It has
an allied Centre of Vocational Studies, which is specifically
designed to develop skills amongst school dropouts and those
who have never attended school.

There remains, however, a great gulf between official
responses to the 'needs' of the modern economy and the
social reality of life in the poor settlements of Kolkata. NGOs,
educational institutions, human rights organisations, activists
in the interest of communal harmony go about their business
with zeal and commitment; yet the impression of separation
is not diminished.

## XVI
## SURVIVAL

In poor people's accounts of their lives in Kolkata, religion
did not feature prominently. Economic and social survival

takes precedence over spiritual considerations. But it does not mean that faith has little or no influence in their lives. The noticeable humanity and restraint of the long-suffering majority in poor settlements are a result of their underlying belief, even though formal observance for many people has lapsed. That they do not provoke violence or disorder – despite the unmerciful conditions in which they are compelled to live – is itself a tribute to the values in which they believe, and by which they try, sometimes against terrible odds, to make a decent life. The most damaged groups – the addicted and the conscienceless – may have forsaken their religion; but most people are guided by faith and trust, which have the ambiguous effect of encouraging them to yield to alterable, human-made injustices, against which revolt would be only too understandable.

Just what the relationship is between this relative quietism of Muslims and the readiness of India's Hindus to throw away so much of their culture for the sake of a disturbed, unquiet consumerism, it is difficult to know; but there is little doubt that the growth of an aggressive Hindutva is in direct proportion to the abandonment of values of austerity, renunciation and reserve; just as the rise in Muslim extremism in the world is, in part, a response to the sybaritic enjoyments of ruling classes everywhere in the Muslim world, and their defiance of modesty and social justice in the practice of Islam.

Poor Muslims have no greater reason than poor Hindus or Christians to define themselves by giving priority to their religion over their humanity; but it remains a basic human need to make sense of life and find meaning in it. We listened to what people told us and, while we heard no story of extremism or fanaticism, most people expressed the cultural and ethical values of a Muslim piety, muted perhaps by poverty and the extinction of social hope. It is not to be doubted that if people are treated with humanity, they will respond in kind. But it is equally obvious that if they are not seen by others as fully human, they will certainly, sooner or later, present themselves in the world, not as they are, but in the light in which others wilfully and perversely perceive them.

And this majority is narrowing the spaces for autonomy and freedom for Muslims in India – and not only in the raucous triumphalism of Narendra Modi's Gujarat – a state governed by the communal Bharatiya Janata Party, which has had repeated electoral success for its overtly anti-Muslim rhetoric and actions. Even as governments announce initiatives and programmes and policies that will 'empower' 'backward' Muslims, their efforts are thwarted by another, more powerful consciousness, inflected by a geo-political separation of Muslims from others, and nourished by war in Iraq, Afghanistan, and threats to Iran, Yemen and Somalia, states pronounced 'failed' by the powerful of the earth. In this context, the old wound of Partition, which never healed, is inflamed and excited once more. What amputee does not dream of being made whole again?

This helps create the culture of official impunity in India wherever Muslims are objects of injustice. Whenever some criminal outrage occurs, the omniscience of the authorities after the event is breathtaking. The police instantly know which group committed the crime and why, which 'outfit' they belong to, where the come from, how they arrived at the site of the atrocity and who their paymasters are. They are swift to produce perpetrators who may or may not – like Aftab Ansari – be involved. If their post hoc intelligence is so good, it is impossible not to wonder why they are unable to prevent the bombings or attacks in the first place.

It seems that the light from the conflagration in Kashmir has irradiated with its lurid colours Muslims all over India: Kashmir, which began as a symbol of a pluralist India, has now become the very opposite; and the blood and grief that have flooded Kashmir since Independence have overflowed and stained the consciousness of India itself.

It is difficult not to marvel at the forbearance and patience of the people of Topsia, Tiljala and Tangra; rather than stigmatising them as dangerous, much could be learned from their honesty and tenacity by those who like to think of themselves as superior to these, their suffering fellow-creatures. In any case, the situation in these poor communities is scarcely stable: change, often violent and coercive, assails them in spite of themselves – yet another reason for seeking refuge in conservative values. It is unreasonable to expect the patient submission of the poor to last for ever, particularly in a country which is richer than it has ever been, and which distributes its resources less and less fairly; so that poor urban Muslims are in perpetual retreat, confined in Kolkata to a restricted and declining proportion of the city's land and the even more straitened terrain of the country's heart.

## XVII
## THE CENTRE FOR OBJECTIVE STUDIES

Dr M. K. A. Siddiqui runs the Institute of Objective Studies from an unpretentious old-fashioned office in the centre of Kolkata. Rows of books are protected from the dust in glass-fronted cupboards; papers on the desk held in place by paperweights flutter in the wind from the fan. Dr Siddiqui used to work with the Anthropological Survey of India, and joined the Centre – which was founded in 1987 – when he retired from government service in 1996. The objective studies are in the interests of communal harmony, a task made no easier by the drift – or is it a drive? – towards Muslim apartness. Among anthropological research quoted by Dr Siddiqui is an investigation into the blood-groups of such apparently diverse communities as Pathans in Waziristan and Nagar Brahmins on the West coast of India. They turn out to have identical blood groups; absolutely no physical distinction exists between them, despite the social and national distance that appears to separate them.

Dr Siddiqui has been particularly concerned with the Muslims who occupy the transitional area of Kolkata, between the central business district and the middle-class residential areas. These, in turn, give way to the upper class districts and an exurban commuter zone. This land belonged originally to Hindu zamindars. Muslims never owned land in the city. With the coming to power of the Left government, the Government took over ownership of the land, effectively becoming zamindars, or landowners of the city. This, paradoxically, for a long time froze construction and maintained the slums of the areas, where 80 per cent of Kolkata's Muslims live. They are essentially pensioners of government-become-landlord. Many of the original structures have been re-built in recent years, in contravention of the law, but in fact in collusion with political and business elites. Reconstruction took place in a very restricted space, so that now, five people typically share between 50 and 100 square feet.

Dr Siddiqui says, 'There is little opportunity for the Muslims to rise. Although they make up over 25 per cent of the population of West Bengal, they have only 2 per cent of government jobs. This contrasts with the general perception, which is that Muslims comprise a far greater proportion of the population than they in fact do – it is common to hear people assert that one-third or even a half of the population of Kolkata is Muslim.

Muslims live by handicrafts – zari-work [embroidery], shoe-making, rubber goods, tailoring. Over time, governments have tried to dislodge Muslims from some of these niches, and they succeeded in ousting them from glassmaking and from soap-making, both traditional Muslim crafts. But Muslims still dominate in some areas – the making of envelopes, diaries and office files – goods associated with clerical work are still in Muslim hands. Of course, most of the artefacts made by Muslims pass through the hands of middlemen, who effectively rob them of the full benefit of their labour. A worker who produces an exquisite embroidery will get 200 rupees, but it will appear in the shop priced at 1,200 rupees or more.

After the report of the Sachar Committee, it was generally acknowledged that help needs to be given to Muslims, artisans and craft-workers as well. Marketing centres are needed that will help them keep a greater proportion of the wealth they earn. For 40 years I have been trying to write and make people understand. Unfortunately, the media are irresponsible in their coverage of issues affecting Muslims. Whatever modest economic gains have been made by Muslims, there is no doubt we have lived through a social recession: Muslim literacy is now lower than it was at the time of Independence. The persistently negative view of the majority in India distorts the self-image of Muslims. For one thing, polygamy among Muslims is lower than it is among Hindus, but who knows that? Sometimes, we absorb not only our own myths and tales, but also those of other people. People sometimes say to me 'The Parsees, who are a small minority, could produce a Tata. You people, what could you do? Poor Muslims do not even know that theirs is a culture of poverty. Does the fish know it is living in water?'

We have real apprehensions about the future. In part because of communal feeling created by the British, we are so distant from education that we have little influence. Hindu communal organisations also exploit this disadvantage. They feed global myths about the increase in the Muslim population, the radicalisation of Muslims, they distort the meaning of Islam. We also have to struggle harder. Hopelessness is against my religion.

But when you look at the reality of Kolkata, it is not encouraging. Only 4 per cent of Muslim children of school-going age in these inner-city communities were actually going to school in 1997. Even when you take into account madrasas and private schools, the total was still less than 10 per cent. Of those, 80 per cent dropped out before Class X, that is, the age of 15.[15]

The majority of children of an age to go to school are child labour, although many now combine this with some schooling. In the last decade, numbers going to school have increased, but it is still pitifully below what it should be. Teaching posts that affect Muslim children are kept vacant, for instance Urdu and Arabic teachers. Every year, teachers are recruited and sit for the exam, so it is not as though there were no qualified teachers. Then the Government says, 'No, these posts are reserved for Scheduled Castes or Scheduled Tribes.' But they know that no one from that group is going to learn Urdu or Arabic, so this becomes another way of denying children's right to education. When you ask them why these posts cannot be de-reserved, or set aside for Muslims under Other Backward Caste groups, they say, 'Oh no, we have to change the law. And that is impossible, because no one in the state legislative Assembly is prepared to bring forward such a bill.'

## XVIII
## INDIA'S GAZA

A young Muslim activist said to me,

These slums are India's Gaza. There is no visible prison, but that does not mean these places are free. Mobility is not prevented by check points, military posts and armed guards; but the exit from misery, ignorance and want is policed by discrimination and prejudice, and these are not tender custodians of borders. It is not by accident that the Indian government is collaborating so much with the state of Israel. We are convinced their deliberations go far beyond defence or trade contracts. Who knows what stories they share with each other on the mysterious arts of institutionalised oppression?

I am neither Indian nor Muslim, but I share with friends who are, a sense of the mindless cruelty and the unnecessary suffering that are tolerated, even encouraged, by governments imprisoned, whether reluctantly or voluntarily, by majoritarian intolerance. To add knowingly to the misery of the poor, whether that of Adivasis, Dalits, Muslims or any other oppressed groups, in the name of 'development', economic success, or in the interests of projecting an image of India as a superpower of tomorrow, is a visitation not to be borne; for it serves a version of India that is a figment, in which most people simply do not recognise the daily pain of their own unacknowledged effort to survive.

# 8
# Postscript: A Servant's Story

Mohammad Irfan is in his mid-50s. He is thin, clean-shaven, with short greying hair; an unobtrusive, gentle man with sincere light-brown eyes. He was born in Bihar in 1953. In the mid-1960s, his parents, landless and impoverished, migrated to East Pakistan with many other Biharis who, disillusioned with India, thought they could, by an act of choice, make good the accident of geography that had stranded them in a country apparently indifferent to the welfare of its Muslim minority. They had, in any case, seen communal riots and feared for their safety. Mohammad Irfan was twelve. His grandmother was sick and could not leave the village. It was agreed he would stay back, and the old woman and the child would take care of each other.

Mohammad Irfan never went to school. He worked from childhood as a day labourer, and with his small income, he and his grandmother lived quietly for about 18 months. She died in 1966, and the boy was alone. He had heard nothing from his parents in East Pakistan. He was 13 years old. An uncle who lived in Kolkata was informed of what had happened, and neighbours looked after Mohammad Irfan until his relative came to fetch him. He had 27 rupees, which his grandmother had buried in the floor in a piece of cloth. He had never worn shoes.

His uncle lived close to Park Circus, but worked as a driver for a middle class family in Salt Lake. He found work for Mohammad Irfan as a live-in servant with a lawyer. Mohammad Irfan says,

> At that time, people in Kolkata did not ask whether you were Hindu or Muslim. If you were willing to work, that was enough, and the family my uncle worked for said that he was reliable and honest. Within a week of arrival in Kolkata, I was a domestic, waiting on a family with two boys close to my own age. I was pleased. I thought they would be company for me, although I was afraid, because they were rich.

The children made sure he understood his subordinate position. They expected him to wait on them, bullied and mistreated him. He had to pick up their clothes, tidy up their things, keep their room clean and 'play' with them, even when that meant riding on his back as though he were an animal. The parents were too busy to notice, although they were not unkind to him. Mohammad Irfan was very unhappy: the children mocked his ignorance and he was also made to feel inferior, so much so that he ceased to observe his religion.

When he complained to his uncle, the uncle said this was his fate, and that he was lucky to have work. As time went by, his employer arranged for him to learn to drive. By the age of 19, driving had become his main job. Life became easier. The boys went to university. One became a chemist, the other a mathematician. The elder was very clever, and after a posting in a university in Orissa, he was offered an academic position in the American mid-West. The second also emigrated, although he did not pursue his academic career in the United States.

Over the years, Mohammad Irfan became indispensable to the depleted household. The lawyer's wife missed her children, and travelled back and forth to the United States. Mohammad Irfan became not only the driver, but also a kind of unofficial companion to his employer. He used to prepare meals and look after the house, as well as supervise the housekeeping. Little by little, even when the lawyer's wife was at home, he still took charge of the household. He never married. He says his duties were his bride. He learned to read and write a little, but his life was more or less devoted to the family he served.

The boys came home to India only occasionally. They still treated Mohammad Irfan as they always had, and their father now sometimes reprimanded them. The elder had married a woman from Kolkata, but the other had an American wife. This woman and her children visited once, but they did not like India. When the lawyer's wife died in 1995, the children came for the funeral, but then ceased coming at all. They invited their father to join them, but he said he was too old to uproot himself, and in any case, his life was in Kolkata.

The lawyer, now in his 70s, became dependent upon Mohammad Irfan. He had a stroke and became partly paralysed. Every day, Mohammad Irfan walked with him in the park. The old man held on to his servant, and learned to walk a little. Mohammad Irfan slept on a mat outside his employer's door, so that if he wanted anything in the night, or if he cried out, he would hear him. Mohammad Irfan says he never slept soundly, because he was always alert in case of need. The old man had become estranged from his sons. They led busy lives. They did not even call. Any contact, even by telephone, had to be initiated by him.

It was only when he had decided to 'adopt' Mohammad Irfan as his son, that they responded. Out of the blue, they arrived at Kolkata airport, and descended on the house in a state of great agitation. They accused the servant of exploiting an elderly man. They said he was taking advantage of his forgetfulness to get money from him, and of poisoning him against his own flesh and blood, cheating them of their rightful inheritance. They were abusive and said they blamed their father for imagining that a Muslim, any Muslim, could be trusted. This hurt Mohammad Irfan more than anything else – he had put up with much unkindness and harshness from the boys, who were by this time about 50.

Mohammad Irfan had been orphaned by the migration of his parents, a desertion which wounded him deeply and destroyed his trust in others. But over the years, he had grown attached to the old man. Nothing could have been further from his mind than the cunning they attributed to him. There was no question that he would remain in the house. In any case, they were taking their father with them to Illinois, so they could care for him in his last years. The father's wishes were easily overruled. The house was sold, Mohammad Irfan dismissed instantly. They gave him 1 lakh rupees. When he protested that he would prefer to remain, if they left their father in his care, they threatened to go to the police and complain that the servant had robbed and cheated their father.

His uncle dead, and with no close relatives, Mohammad Irfan wanders the city, a melancholy wraith-like man, dignified but bitter that his years of service should have been so misunderstood. He says he re-lives every day the moment when he was turned out of the house that had been his home for almost 40 years. Towards the end, the old man was suffering from memory loss, and he was in no position to thwart the plans of his sons. Mohammad Irfan does not know whether the old man is still alive. He was taken to America in 2005. Mohammad Irfan still goes back to look at the house. It is now altered, has been modernised and re-painted. Mohammad Irfan pays rent to his cousin, his uncle's daughter and her husband. He has shelter, but lacks purpose. He asked me if I were married, and when I said no, he offered to come and look after me; that he did so after just an hour's conversation in a Kolkata park suggested the depth of his despair. A year later, I saw him again. This time, he did not recognise me, and I let him pass without reminding him of the moment of sad intimacy we had shared.

## CONCLUSION

The communities where we stayed, unvisited by wealth or power, are places imagined by the powerful, who believe that pollution, conspiracy and over-population make them dangerous places. They are solemnly said by those who have never been there to be sites of vice and iniquity, breeding grounds for a vast reservoir of demonic humanity – the 'haunts' of criminals, goondas, extortioners, but also of terrorists, ultras, militants, extremists, infiltrators. They are toxic dumps for the prejudices of new dominant castes in India – among whom are merchants of hatred, dealers in bad faith, speculators in prejudice, traffickers in acrimony and discord; commodities intangible but highly profitable in a time of fearful and driven social change. The new middle class, suffering all the nervous disorders of a society caught up in the exaltations of 'development' and sudden riches project their fears onto the perishing inhabitants of wanting neighbourhoods like Topsia, Tiljala Road and Tangra. Poor Muslims thus become victims of a reckless social wastage, a squandering of human resources, just as so much of their labour is uselessly expended on a pitiable rescue-mission of the garbage among which they live.

# Notes

1. *Basti* is from the Hindi, 'basana', to dwell or set up home. It is defined as a 'congested settlement with a high population density, having grown in an unplanned manner, and facing problems of infrastructural deficiency. Sometimes the word is used for slum.' Amitabh Kundu and Somnath Basu, UNESCO Management and Social Transformation Programme, Working Paper No. 4, December 1999.

2. The Sachar Committee was set up by the Manmohan Singh government in 2005 to look into the social, economic and educational position of Muslims in India. It reported at the end of 2006. It found literacy among Muslims well below the national average, especially in urban areas and among women. A quarter of Muslim children aged between 6 and 14 years have either never been to school or have dropped out. Muslims are poorly represented in professional and managerial classes. Average bank-loans to Muslims are only two-thirds of the amount disbursed to other minorities. Villages which are predominantly Muslim are particularly ill served, both by infrastructure and educational facilities. In the IAS, only 3 per cent of employees are Muslim; in the IFS 1.8 per cent and in IPS 4 per cent. Indian Railways employees are 4.5 per cent Muslim, but the vast majority are in lower positions. Muslims are seriously under-represented in universities and banks.

   In an attempt to combat some of the myths about Muslims, Sachar found that only 4 per cent of Muslim children study in madrasas, and these do so mainly because of an absence of functioning government schools. Muslim fertility has declined significantly, contrary to propaganda that Muslims are conspiratorially 'breeding' in order to outnumber Hinds. Muslims complained of being doubly castigated, for being 'anti-national' on the one hand, and for having to be 'appeased' on the other.

The Sachar Committee proposed the setting up of an Equal Opportunity Commission, a national data bank, a process for evaluating textbooks, and a system of allocation of university and college places that reflect the composition of the local population.

3. The Report of the National Commission for Religious and Linguistic Minorities, under Justice Ranganath Misra, reported in 2007. Among its principal recommendations were that 15 per cent of places in government services and seats in educational establishments should be reserved for Muslims; and that 8.48 per cent of the existing Other Backward Classes quota of 27 per cent should be reserved for minorities. It stressed that the basis for reservation should be social and economic backwardness.

4. Hearing these stories reminded me of a tale I had heard in the North of England in the 1970s, when it was regularly asserted that poor people, especially, in this instance, Roman Catholics, recklessly produced large families they could not maintain. One elderly man said, 'I heard my neighbour saying how irresponsible it was to have big families. I had eight children. I said to him, "Just wait a minute will you?" I called all my children into the garden and stood them in line. Then I said to him, "Now, look at these, and tell me which ones I ought not to have had."'

5. Illich, Ivan, *H2O and the Waters of Forgetfulness*, London: Marion Boyars, 1986.

6. See Siddiqui, Dr M. K. A., *Social and Cultural Empowerment of Muslims in India*. New Delhi: Institute of Objective Studies, 2009.

7. *Times of India*, 30 December 2007.

8. *The Telegraph*, Kolkata, 31 December 2007.

9. Interview given by Amartya Sen, *The Telegraph*, 23 July 2007.

10. UN-Habitat, The Challenge of Slums, 2003.

11. Siddiqui, Dr M.K.A, *Life in the Slums of Kolkata*. New Delhi: Genuine Publications & Media Pvt., 1997.

12. Ibid.

13. *The Telegraph*, Kolkata, 23 February 2005.

14. AIDOS is an inspired name for the Italian organisation, Associazione Italiana Donne per lo Sviluppo (The Association of Italian Women

for Development), since Aidos was the name of the Greek goddess of humility and modesty. The word also connotes a feeling of shame of the rich in the presence of poverty. The organisation has been helping to fund education for girls in Tiljala since 1995, partly by compensating the families for earnings foregone. In the first ten years, 136 girls were individually sponsored; and this has been a contributory factor in Tiljala to the heightened appreciation of girls' education in the area. More than two-thirds of the sponsored girls were studying between Class VI and X, 10 per cent in Class XI and XII, while 6 per cent had gone on to further education.

15. These figures refer to the mid-1990s. Since that time, there has certainly been an increase in the numbers of Muslim children attending school in the inner-city areas of Kolkata – the school of Shaikh Shamsher Alam in Topsia alone will have had some small statistical impact. But no published figures exist.

## KEEP IN TOUCH WITH PLUTO PRESS

For special offers, author updates, new title info and more there are plenty of ways to stay in touch with Pluto Press.

Our Website: http://www.plutobooks.com

Our Blog: http://plutopress.wordpress.com

Our Facebook: http://www.facebook.com/PlutoPress

Our Twitter: http://twitter.com/plutopress

 **Pluto**Press
www.plutobooks.com